Beginner's Guide to Shorecasting

Beginner's Guide to Shorecasting

Ray Forsberg

With 41 drawings by BAZ EAST

PELHAM BOOKS

First published in Great Britain by
PELHAM BOOKS LTD
52 Bedford Square
London WC1B 3EF
1974

ISBN 0 7207 0753 6

Set and printed in Great Britain by
Tonbridge Printers Ltd, Peach Hall Works, Tonbridge, Kent
in Times eleven on twelve point on paper supplied by
P. F. Bingham Ltd, and bound by James Burn
at Esher, Surrey

Contents

Illustrations

Introduction

This is essentially a book about escapism; getting away from the irksome, mundane chores of life and 'opting out'. Down on the shoreline, where the fishing is almost always free, the air bracing, the surf exhilarating and the solitude (especially at night under the stars) a wonderful relaxing tonic which soothes taut nerves that have for too long been 'jangled' by the fearsome pace of modern life.

Everything I have learned in more than forty years of continuous shore walking, tide watching, bait digging and all-weather fishing has been gathered together in these pages to put the prospective 'Shorecaster' immediately on to the right track so far as his tackle, bait, bodily comfort, footwear, accessories and personal safety are concerned.

The seashore (except in a very few places) is ours to fish and enjoy as we please – night or day – the whole year round. Until you have seen the sea in all its many moods, throughout all the seasons, stood still and very much alone in the darkness with a rod in your hand; gutted your catch in the shallow surf and returned home healthily tired from a long session on a very remote and peaceful shoreline, to cook and eat with the utmost relish really fresh fish ... You have not yet begun to live.

But it is never ever too late to start – and this book will show you how.

9

CHAPTER ONE

The Shorecasting Scene Today

'The last, almost impregnable stronghold of angling freedom' is an apt, if somewhat optimistic, description of the saltwater fishing to be had along the many miles of varied coastline which continuously fringe the British Isles.

As each new day produces a fresh crop of irritating problems which constantly bedevil the poor, long-suffering coarse and game (salmon and trout) fisherman, the shorecasters' domain – that fascinating 'free-to-all' Tom Tiddler's Ground between the tide lines, much loved by anglers, naturalists, beachcombers and seabirds – remains just a little more immune from the ever increasing ravages of present-day life.

Apart from direct industrial pollution, dumping, filling-in and agricultural seepage, as well as the odd chemical or oil-carrying road tanker which skids off the tarmac and deposits its obnoxious cargo into some exclusive angling club's treasured trout stream, the freshwater angler who rents a stretch of river, a landscaped gravel pit or a secluded carp pool now has the added financial burden of Value Added Tax to contend with.

In addition to the rapid deterioration of his waters and the ever increasing cost of fishing in them, the coarse fish, salmon, or trout anglers are bound and fettered by senseless, archaic rules, close seasons, bait bans, method restrictions and a general 'shut-down' on the majority of waters during the hours of darkness, neatly and very effectively cuts him off from taking full advantage of some of the most productive periods which his chosen branch of the sport could offer.

Small wonder that the present-day angling trend is a general swing to the free, wide open sea and, in particular, towards the many miles of shoreline which is all around us and never far away. Even if you live well inland it can be reached by car or bus in three or four hours at the most.

While boat fishing generally brings heavier catches, a greater variety of fish and a less energetic way to travel for the angler and his tackle (not to mention the fish on the return journey) there are often long periods of stormy weather, especially during the winter months, when even the all-weather vessels of commercial fishing fleets deem it wise and prudent to stay firmly tied up in harbour. Following their safety first code, the pleasure rod-and-line anglers are also kept ashore – their bait going rapidly 'off' and their nerves becoming more frayed hourly. This is especially so if the trip has been booked and looked forward to well in advance and the fishing party have travelled a fair distance to enjoy a welcome trip 'on the briny', some good sport, and the prospect of a weighty string of fresh fish to top up the fridge at home.

Unfortunately, the sudden boom in boating during the past decade has rocketed the prices of harbour dues, mooring fees and even the payments for the use of slipways and launching equipment, thereby dealing a rather foul body blow to the newcomer to sea angling who fancies his chances as master of his own craft. In certain very popular 'messing-about-in-boat' areas, there is such a heavy saturation of would-be boat owners in addition to those already in operation, that berthing and harbour facilities or even makeshift moorings are at a premium, with long waiting lists which bar the pathway of prospective boat owners who are sufficiently affluent to surmount all the other pocket-hitting pitfalls of private boat ownership.

Gradually the confining barriers which separate the three distinct branches of fishing for pleasure (coarse, sea and game) are being eroded away by higher standards of living, greater amounts of leisure and better personal transport facilities, so that daily, an increasing number of keen, discerning anglers are availing themselves of the best of the fishing to be offered by all three branches of the sport. In particular a great number of hitherto confirmed trout, salmon and coarse fishers are sampling the delights of sea angling and finding it much to their liking. Of course, the pendulum swings both ways and we now have in the 'fishing game' a growing number of all-rounders, accomplished anglers whose fishing calendar is ordered by piscatorial seasons rather than the four generally recognised ones of spring, summer, autumn, and winter. Spring to these 'best-of-the three-worlds of angling' sportsmen means trout and salmon; summer and autumn for coarse fishing; and winter for beach or boat angling, the latter according to the dictates of that overlord of all fishing mariners – the weather.

Three Categories of Shorecasters

Within the confines of the term 'Shorecasters' we find a trio of rather loosely defined groups, as well as three types of shoreline or angling 'station' from which they fish. By far the greatest number of shorecasting sea anglers are those who reside on the coast and avail themselves of whatever kind of fishing presents itself readily in their immediate locality – usually well within walking or cycling distance. The most fortunate of this group live in what I would call 'Heaven-sent, copybook angling situations' with a beach of sand or shingle (steeply shelving for preference); a long pier or harbour wall and some adjacent rock formations giving on to very deep water – angling paradise indeed, with all the three types of fishing stations mentioned earlier.

The keen sea anglers who are blessed with such a wealth of fishing and variation of venue right on their very doorstep invariably become so enamoured with the whole business of shorecasting, bait digging, weather and tide watching and tackle making, that their whole lives revolve around it and a fanatical few who are personally known to me even adjust their working hours – as they are self-employed – so that absolutely nothing interferes with their pursuit of good sport.

In such ideal angling circumstances, once the initial outlay for tackle; certain necessary items of weatherproof clothing; a reliable night-light and a good digging fork has been met, very little further expense is incurred apart from occasional replacements or repairs. The true lone wolf angler, who forms the backbone of the shorecasting fraternity is hardly ever a joiner-of-angling-clubs or organisations. Far from being an angling socialite, he deliberately seeks quiet shores, isolated rocky headlands and a place on the pier or harbour wall in the middle of the night when it is likely to be deserted. He revels in being completely independent and pitting his wits and skill against the wind, the weather and the sea in order to reap a rich, but often very hard won, harvest of the fish that swim therein.

The Local Angler

Over the course of the years, this kind of sea angler who sticks to his own little patch or stamping-ground and very rarely travels far afield for his sport, has been termed a 'local', and his tackle, bait, and angling methods will usually be confined to what has been tried, tested and found to be successful by generations of his angling forebears.

A very good example of how traditional shorecasting tackle has remained almost static in design and development can be found along the Yorkshire coast, where a very hardy breed of rock anglers fish from ledges and cast into the roughest of kelp tangles with what is known as 'Scarborough Tackle'. A 9–10 ft. 'stout pole' originally of greenheart or double-built cane, but now modernised to hollow glass, is used in conjunction with the far famed 'Scarborough' reel (fearsome in the hands of a novice) which is a one-piece, gearless, turned-wood or 'Tuffnol' wheel about 7 in. in diameter, mounted on a brass bracket with two large winding knobs on which your knuckles can be skinned if you make a false move while casting.

Sceptical visitors to the North Yorkshire coast around the Whitby, Scarborough, Filey Brig and Flamborough areas are apt to scoff when they see anglers using extra strong nylon monofilament lines around the breaking strain mark of 60, 70 or even 80 lb. with heavy spoon-shaped leads and the rod and reel described. However, they are soon convinced of its effectiveness as the right tackle to beat the snags, and the fish, which have to be 'pulley-hauled' through the jungle of weed, and also winched as a suspended weight up through the air, kicking and struggling, to where the angler is perched, perhaps 50, 100, or even 200 ft. above water level. To punish an expensive multiplier reel and a lightweight beach-casting rod by using it for such a gruelling task would be angling sacrilege, which clearly points the way towards an open, receptive mind in all matters appertaining to tackle and methods when an unfamiliar venue is being 'scouted' and the local anglers observed in action for the first time.

The Competitive Angler

In direct contrast to the shorecasting recluse who revels in solitude and lonely places; the 'match-fishing' sea angler is a much more gregarious, often flamboyant personality, whose ego is boosted to the skies when he pits his wits and skill against his fellow human competitors in addition to the finned opponents which fight him on the other end of his line.

While the lone wolf local shore angler is primarily interested in the fish he catches from a 'how will it go with chips' eating point of view, the 'Shorecasting Match' or 'Fishing Festival' exponent's chief concern is to put a goodly weight of something fishy on to the scales at weigh-in time, so that the culinary quality of his catch is liable to be of secondary importance.

The giants of the 'All Comer's Sea Angling Championships' and 'Open Shore Contest' world usually begin their competitive fishing apprenticeship as good all-rounders and gradually launch themselves into the limelight after being attracted to organised sea angling matches in their own little area. These they usually win easily, much to the dismay of the 'outsiders' who enter and fail to fish the allotted beach marks with the right bait or tackle.

With a few cups on the sideboard, a brand new colour

T.V. for the kids, and a fridge for the little woman slaving in the kitchen – not to mention perhaps a couple of hundred pounds in ready tax-free cash from prize money – all gained from match fishing wins – the top-dog sea match angler very soon begins to feel his feet. He equips himself with a comprehensive set of expensive gear, he studies the coastline, tackle and methods at places far afield and sets out his stall to become a widely travelled journeyman sea angler of the very highest order.

Successful sea match angling is, however, far from being all glamour, prizes, sweepstake money and newspaper photographs. Behind every good match-winning performance which may last for just five or six hours; there may have been days, or even weeks of preparation on the part of the winning participant, who has perhaps into the bargain, travelled a round trip journey of five or six hundred miles in order to compete.

To see a 'big turnout' sea angling match in progress with anywhere between 1,500 and 2,000 anglers of all shapes, sizes, temperaments, tackle preferences and angling styles, strung out along many miles of coastline, is indeed an education which no prospective 'on the brink' sea angler can afford to miss. The baits, terminal gear, casting techniques, rods, reels, personal apparel, tackle boxes and seating accommodation (if any) are legion, and much better seen in use under actual fishing conditions, rather than resting all new and shiny with a formidable price-tag in the showcase of the tackle shop.

This business of getting a free 'in action' preview of every item which is used in angling, is a very wise procedure which any sea angling newcomer should be recommended to follow. Whilst dealer's catalogues, leaflets and tackle-trade handouts give very useful details of the construction, finish, price range, technical design and suggested uses; practising anglers who possess such items and have them in continuous use are a very sound authority on how the product *really* performs for fish catching, and above all, what sort of period can be reckoned as its useful, trouble-free life, provided it is given proper care and usage.

The Specialist

The final and third group of our shorecasting types is the 'Sea Specimen Hunter', 'Record Fish Seeker' or 'Exclusive Species Angler'. Perhaps these definitions are a little bewildering and need some clarification. When the coarse fishing scene in this country was suddenly transformed about 1950 by just a handful of forward-thinking innovators who brought about a revolution in tackle, methods, baits and angling approach, there appeared on the rivers, lakes, streams and ponds certain highly disciplined anglers whose sole aim was to concentrate on the capture of the largest specimens of whatever species they chose to pursue: carp, roach, barbel, pike or chub; to name but a few. To the exclusion of all other fish, they firmly fixed their sights on record breakers and were content to tread a very lonely, arduous path in order to achieve their ambitions. Somewhere along the line (pardon my angling-flavoured pun) with the free interchange of ideas in all branches of fishing, a good hefty injection of the specimen hunting spirit was pumped into the sea anglers' veins and naturally it became the vogue to be a specialist whose thoughts seemed to dwell continually on perhaps monster bass, huge cod, or even shore-caught conger eels of frightening size!

Some 'local' anglers and quite a few match fanatics immediately fell under the spell of this 'big fish' approach to sea angling and began to study the habits of whatever species took their fancy and also to experiment with rods, reels, terminal tackles, baits and methods which would take them. Not content with fishing the shores in their area; especially if the fish they sought were liable to be thin over the ground; they began to travel extensively, especially at week-ends and while on holiday, for the precise purpose of being able to fish all the venues which were recognised as being capable of producing fish of near record size of the species which held their interest.

Although it is most convenient for shorecasting events which attract a great number of far-travelled anglers to be held during the hours of daylight; the sea angling specialist pays little attention to the night- and day-time factor when he is considering an outing. The tides and the state of the weather are his sole interest. Also, of considerable importance: he likes to view the prospective shoreline at low water and study it carefully, mapping out and often measuring, by walking paces, the distance from dead low water to the highest 'tide mark' which is usually shown by a line of dried-out seaweed and rubbish, well up the beach.

I am quite certain that the development of general sea fishing (and especially shorecasting) tackle would have been very slow indeed had it not been for the constant striving for perfection in design and materials, and of great importance, preoccupation with lightness, that has been made by the sea specimen hunting fraternity, with the laurels going to a handful of scientifically-minded engineers and inventors with a great love of fishing. There is no finer method of arriving at greater angling efficiency – so far as tackle is concerned – than to have the designer, manufacturer and tester all rolled into one person: a practising angler.

Having digressed a little from my original theme which was a survey of angling types and strayed into the realms of fishing tackle design; I will now return to the humans who make up the greater part of the one-and-a-quarter million souls listed as sea anglers by the 1970 National Angling Survey and loosely called 'shore fishers'.

My three separate categories Locals, Sea Contest Anglers, and Specimen Hunters or Specialists, in no way covers every single shore fisher who actively participates in the sport – they merely represent a majority trio. Some shorecasters have a liking for all three types of angling and divide their time equally between fishing their local pier or 'Town' beach on weekdays; journeying far afield to big Open Shore Contests at week-ends and then flying off across the sea to Ireland to fish exclusively for bass during their summer holiday break.

Location Forecasting

The habits of the fish which are to be found within casting range in our inshore waters, their seasonal movements, and above all else, their distribution; are the important deciding factors which govern where, when and how anglers fish in various geographical areas. Before anyone who is contemplating becoming a shorecaster pays a visit to a tackle shop with the intention of purchasing some suitable equipment to get started with, certain vital information must be sought. The sources are large scale Ordnance Survey maps, the local fishing-tackle shop or sea angling club, and by personal observation of anglers who are in action on nearby beaches, piers, jetties, harbour walls and any other vantage points from which fish are taken.

This 'what am I liable to catch' question is a constant conundrum to all anglers who are new to the sport and have not had many years experience in observing different types of shoreline. The sea is not a large pond in which all the fish that swim therein can be caught eventually from one place by sheer persistence. At times I have fished a beach for cod, and due to a complete absence of anything slightly resembling a bite, would have been convinced there were no such fish within a hundred miles; were it not for the fact that I had later seen several small boats which had been fishing just half a mile out from where I stood, come ashore with stones of prime cod littering the bottom boards! On other occasions the reverse has applied, with beach anglers taking bumper bags, and dinghy fishers out beyond the breakers sitting fishless.

As a very rough guide: the north and south-east coast of England from Berwick to the Isle of Wight can be called winter (September to about April) cod fishing ground, with mixed bags which may include flatfish, thornback rays, tope, bass, coalfish and mackerel at certain places during the summer months – but at other venues a veritable host of bait-robbing crabs, especially along the Yorkshire coast, which makes warm weather shorecasting intolerable.

Commencing on the East Anglian coast and taking in the whole of the south of England, Cornwall, and the coast of Wales, bass can be expected in summer; but as in all angling, nothing can be predicted as a dead certainty, therefore no hard and fast rules can ever be made about when fish should appear close inshore and then depart again.

The whole trouble with the fish location forecasting business is that certain very thinly populated areas which have very few, if any, shore anglers, do not appear on the distribution lists, maps, charts or species tables. Scotland is a typical case in point where whole areas are virgin, unfished ground, the shorecasting potential of which is completely untapped and hardly ever 'written up' or reported in the angling press.

A cursory glance through one or two of the older sea angling books (pre-1960) will give a clear indication that the wrasse can be found almost everywhere around our coasts where there are rocks and weed with deepish water. This cannot be taken literally today as the disastrous 'arctic' winter of 1962–3 killed off huge colonies of them and in certain areas they have to date not yet recovered and reappeared in anything like their former numbers.

Since the advent of concentrated inshore trawling by small vessels fitted with the most up-to-the-moment navigation and fish finding aids, the joyful habit by shore and boat fishing anglers of noising abroad precise details of locations where good catches have been made has been hastily discontinued by those who wish to enjoy their sport and not have it disappear suddenly overnight. If this appears to sound like a stale music-hall joke, I can assure readers that many times after a series of particularly good catches from beaches have been reported in the 'Coastal Report' sections of the angling press, highly elated shorecasters have journeyed there to find the whole area being swept clean by a fleet of shallow-draughted fishing boats trawling within casting distance of the beach.

For a long time sea anglers have been deluded by the false belief that while a flat sandy bottom could be trawled effectively and 'cleaned-out' by commercial fishing, the rougher type of rocky ground was safe habitation for sea fish as it would damage the gear: therefore on balance certain parts of the sea would remain as prolific as ever and fish stocks would never suffer total annihilation. Constant, concentrated 'long-lining' has debunked the 'too rough to trawl' theory with devastating effect.

At the risk of labouring a theme and appearing unnecessarily gloomy; let me quote the case of the thornback ray, which like the wrasse is listed in the older angling books as being found all around the British coast over sand, mud and gravel. Unfortunately stocks of this fish in the North Sea have been of late sadly depleted, they have been given such a 'bashing' from the trawl and long-line commercial 'boys' that certain areas of it are virtually cleaned out of thornbacks and cannot now recover, unless a miracle takes place, and the world of angling and indeed all conservation, seems remarkably short of such happenings at the present time.

The price that has to be paid by all sport fishers around our shores in these days of rapid change, is one of eternal vigilance, so that the needs of the nation's anglers are not hastily pushed into the background when other, seemingly more important matters are at stake. We are a nation of island dwellers surrounded by a continuous shoreline, most of which could provide quite productive fishing if strict pollution control and conservation was considered of paramount importance to the wellbeing of the community; rather than the overawing, greedy god of profit!

With more leisure time in the offing, better personal transport facilities and continuous talk of increasingly earlier retirement, it behoves us all to lean very heavily on the people who at present rather sketchily control our destiny, so that by the time the magical year of 2000 is reached we shall not see ourselves as inhabiting 'an island set in fishless seas'.

CHAPTER TWO

Tackle: What is available

If I have waxed exceeding pessimistic in the last half dozen paragraphs of the previous chapter and plunged my readers into deep despair regarding the ecological decline of our water encompassed environment, let me now raise him (or her: at least two distinguished ladies hold British 'big sea fish' records) right up to a joyous in-the-clouds level by delving deeply into the truly wonderful world of the present-day fishing tackle and accessories scene.

Never has such a wealth of international gear from a truly world-wide source been so freely available as it is right now. No wonder that any new beginner, with his money burning a hole in his pocket, but only a vague idea of what tackle he requires, backs off in dismay when he first enters a large walk-around tackle shop and gazes about him in panic-stricken awe at the hundreds of rods and scores of different reels from which he can make his choice; not to mention waders, hats, coats, electric headlamps and even a small library of angling books!

Perhaps it is Saturday afternoon; the shop is full of customers and the tills are ringing frantically, with assistants and even the proprietor (plus his harassed wife) coping manfully with a spending boom. In such circumstances it would be foolish to expect a conducted tour of the premises with a patient and detailed explanation of every item in stock. You may just possibly get such red carpet treatment if you appeared in that trade depression period immediately after the Christmas rush, but the really intelligent approach to this knotty problem of buying the correct tackle can only be solved by a very thorough study of every tackle catalogue available and many hours of 'browsing' in well stocked shops.

Sources of Information

At the time of writing, there are two weekly angling newspapers on the market: *Angling Times* and *Angler's Mail*; and three monthly magazines: *Angling, Sea Angler* and *Fisherman*; all of which give very full coverage to advertisers who cater specially for the needs of fishermen – be it tackle, clothing, bait, boat trips, holidays, or insurance. From the firms who advertise in the publications listed, can be obtained comprehensive catalogues (some running to a couple of hundred pages – all profusely illustrated) of the items they stock, and the average price of obtaining such a wonderful book of inside information is usually as low as 30p which includes postage.

With half a dozen such books; a big armchair before a roaring fire on a winter's night and unlimited time at your disposal, you can do your angling homework information gathering in comfort, and have a clear picture in your mind what to look for and examine the next time you go on a fact finding tour of a fishing tackle shop.

At the outset: immediately you delve into the pages of your pile of catalogues you will discover that while there are a great many items which do not lend themselves to the Do-It-Yourself approach – those that do are very well catered for so far as the buying of the component parts are concerned. Let me make it crystal clear at this point that the 'homemade' D.I.Y. approach to tackle production is not considered a second best approach in angling, or a cheap alternative to a manufactured article. Provided the very best materials are used, it is the only way to obtain a tailored-to-taste, exclusive-design item of tackle which would otherwise cost a small fortune to have specially made by a high-class craftsman.

A circumspect survey of the rods listed in the catalogues will reveal that while the trout and salmon (game) fishers still use a few rods made up of 'split' built cane and so also to a lesser extent do coarse fishermen; the sea anglers, especially shorecasters, use rods in solid and hollow glass and very little else. The only exceptions are a few old stagers who still cling to those 'ton heavy' ancient greenheart barge poles, unreliable 'Burma Canes' and unbelievably heavy and thick double-built cane weapons with immense, weighty, solid brass reel fittings and ferrules, enormous rings and great long cork handles.

Solid and hollow glass rod 'blanks' (the pieces from which the rods are made) can be purchased in a variety of lengths, tapers and qualities. The cheapest two-piece 12 ft. solid glass set, for a general 'knockabout' beach rod will cost three or four pounds, and so on up to the extra special, thin walled, steep taper, rod blank set for about ten or twelve pounds. With the addition of good rings, vinyl handgrips and a lightweight reel fitting and ferrules this will make up into a custombuilt rod at less than half the price of the ready-made article.

With such a huge tackle buying turnover which has been brought about by greatly increased spending power among anglers, there is a constant flow of sound, little used gear on to the second-hand market. Rod and reel manufacturers just love introducing new models as often as they possibly can so that they keep their customers happily buying each year's latest product, fondly believing that to fish with 'dated' gear is rather outmoded and psychologically damaging to the ego. To tackle buyers with well lined pockets, I say 'keep buying' – it is healthy for trade, and to those who are somewhat low in funds my advice is: swallow your pride and rather than buy a cheap new item of tackle, go every time for a betterclass second-hander, provided it is in very good condition.

A long time ago, in the Hungry 'Thirties, when I grew up – which makes me feel very ancient – fishing tackle shops, except those which catered solely for the out and out 'toffs', only sold fishing tackle. What the angler wore was of no concern to them simply because after stretching his budget to the limit there was never any spare money left for personal apparel. Old working clothes were called into use for seashore and riverbank, which is why the tremendous rift developed between the gentlemen 'flay fish-ahs' all resplendent in special fishing togs, and the down-at-heel, skulking, greasy mufflered, tatty overcoated, 'flat-'atted' coarse and sea types.

It is with immense pleasure that I now say that all such nonsense has long been swept away, as evidence by the glorious range of anglers' clothing and accessories which the fishing tackle shops are now stocking. This business of being a fishing tackle dealer is becoming more of a specialised profession every day, and those who do not keep their knowledge of tackle developments abreast of the times; their angling skills highly polished; and their heads jam-packed with all the angling news, fall miserably by the wayside and relinquish their customers to other competitive 'live wires' whose shops always seem full to overflowing with discerning fishermen who are cheerfully prepared to travel many miles for the very best in tackle, first class bait, reliable after-sales service and sound advice and guidance at all times.

Top class fishing tackle dealers; the ones who fish regularly themselves and draw their staff from practising anglers; pride themselves on taking into stock only such items as they themselves have thoroughly tested and can recommend. Each new face which appears in their premises could be either a 'once only' customer, or a 'solid regular' whose annual business may run to three or four hundred pounds. Such clients need to be nursed very carefully and never ever sold faulty, unreliable or unsuitable gear. However, despite the fact that the man behind the counter is trying his level best to give you a good deal – the final choice is always yours, right or wrong.

To shortcut the whole business and endeavour to eliminate the pitfalls of this tackle choice dilemma, one very enterprising Scandinavian tackle firm has evolved a '1 to 4' code 'balanced tackle' system, with four different colours representing approximate line strength ranges and casting weights. Their comprehensive tackle chart makes the choice of matching up a rod and reel very simple; the line strength ratings and casting weight figures also remove any doubts from the buyers mind as to what is the most suitable weight of lure, bait or lead which the rod, reel and suggested line strength will most successfully cast, play fish and generally perform with.

Without fail, each time I go on a fishing trip to the coast, I see at least one angler using some item of tackle for a purpose which it was never intended by the designer and manufacturer and punishing it most heartlessly in the process. Quite a lot of this shocking bad management on the part of inexperienced anglers can be prevented by buying all tackle from a reputable dealer who will always be most willing to advise on the particular article which is being purchased.

Mail order firms who produce a bumper catalogue full of clothing, household articles and a selection of sports equipment – which includes fishing tackle – are a source of great annoyance to all fishing tackle dealers, as it is they who are called upon to sort out the problems of wrongly selected articles, after-sales service and even that age old dilemma 'I can't understand the instruction book – can you show me how it works?'

Although generally, proprietary brands of fishing gear can be obtained in all parts of the country; the tackle shops in certain areas do tend to stock what is most suitable for use in their special locality and the tackle dealers themselves – the good ones I mean – who naturally fish in their free time, almost always become 'local' experts, whose advice is much sought after and acted upon by all angling beginners who visit them for their initial tackle outfit.

Differing Requirements

The three different types of shorecasting station of which I wrote in chapter one, are all liable to demand a completely separate approach so far as the angler's energy, dress, amount of equipment and type of tackle are concerned. For instance, a retired angler in his late sixties, whose sole interest will be warm weather angling from the local pier, to which 'fishing station' he drives sedately in his car, parking it only a few yards away from where he is fishing, will not need all the weather-beating clothing which is vitally important to the all-weather shorecasting angler who stands out at night in half a gale on an exposed beach.

To quote another instance for which a different set of angling clothing, tackle carrier, footwear and fishing gear would be needed; let us consider the all-weather, pier or harbour wall angler and the roving 'rock station' fisherman. The first static type of angling practised from a safe, dry, firm footing with no long walks or clambering involved, could be done in great comfort from a lightweight, portable camp chair in the very warmest of thick waterproof clothes, masses of sweaters and fur-lined boots with gloves and hat as well in the same material if required. Two rods, supported on heavy-duty metal tripods could be operated quite successfully, and if, as I have seen on some piers and harbour walls, car parking was allowed, then the fortunate angler could luxuriate inside his heater-warmed vehicle, sipping thermos flask tea and listening to 'Top-of-the-Pops' on his car radio – all the time of course, keeping a watchful eye on his rods!

But what of the 'Rock Hopper?' The gear just described would have him staggering under the weight of it (two rods with heavy tripods) not to mention the 'overweight clothing' in which he would only be able to scramble a few hundred yards before he was in a chill-producing lather and worn out from the sheer fatigue of wearing it! His watchword must be 'lightweight everything', with the absolute maximum amount of freedom and movement of his legs and arms – rather like a mountaineering angler in fact. To keep him as free-handed as possible, a roomy, well-fitting pack or rucksack would be his ideal way of carrying all his tackle, and it is vital that his footwear is suitable for the rock surfaces (wet, dry and 'suicide-green' weedy) over which he will travel. Those beautiful, expensive green thigh waders, in the thinnest, most supple material, would certainly appear to be ideal for keeping him dry shod, but a few minutes of grappling himself over and in between barnacle studded rocks would quickly tear them to shreds.

From those few observations on the suitability of clothing

and tackle carrying gear, it will be obvious that for certain types of fishing it is a wise course of action when considering the gathering together of the equipment, to send off for not only a fishing tackle dealer's catalogues; but a couple from a mountaineering supplies or outdoor life and camping shop as well!

Specially for the Sea Fisherman
To conclude this chapter, and before I go on to deal with rods, reels and other items of equipment in separate chapters in which I will fully describe them and explore their uses, will briefly run through the contents of the 'Sea Fishing Section' of an average dealer's catalogue, always bearing in mind that there are certain items in the 'Coarse Fishing' and 'Fly Fishing' sections which lend themselves admirably to the sea fisher, provided he takes the utmost precautions with all the metal parts on them which may suffer from that deadly menace – salt water corrosion.

Immediately a prospective rod buyer begins to leaf through any rod specifications lists, he will realise that the average length of what is known in the tackle trade as a 'beachcaster' is 12 ft. (two 6 ft. pieces in fact) a size which is a little too long to fit up the middle between the seats of some of the smaller cars. With this precise stowage problem in mind, at least one enterprising tackle firm has produced a three-piece beachcaster – two hollow glass pieces (top and middle joint) and a separate detachable butt; the overall length of this rod when dismantled is about 4 ft. 6 in. Rod holdalls, for beachcasters, also need to be specially made as the general run of such items designed to hold coarse fishing rods and umbrellas are in sizes 5 ft. and 5 ft. 6 in. Again, a special sea angler's rod holdall has been designed and manufactured which is 6 ft. 4 in. in length, but care must be taken when buying or ordering all rod holdalls that the one purchased will really take the rod for which it is intended – as a 6ft. holdall will not usually take a 12 ft. rod (in two pieces). At least three or four extra inches on the holdall length are necessary so that it can be zipped up with ease.

One other quite unforeseen snag can also be the fact that angling beginners quite often fail to realise that certain reels are fished 'on top of the rod' with rings and reel uppermost (as in the case of multipliers, and certain 'closed-face' spinning and lure-casting reels intended for use on short 'crank-handled' rods), and the rest (fixed-spool, side-cast, and the old-fashioned 'Scarborough' reels) underneath the rod with the rings pointing downwards. A further complication with the 'under or over' rod, is that the majority of multiplier reels are made for right-hand winding – those for left-handers are not always made by some reel manufacturers.

Having more or less disposed of those two small snags concerning the major items of the shorecasters armoury (rod and reel) we will move on to all the other varied and interesting items which are available. Of late, it has become possible to buy nylon monofilament line in bulk spools and some of the fantastic quantities offered do seem to be rock-bottom price bargains. Here a timely word of warning is called for, which will save the shorecasting tyro much heartache in his tackle buying. Cheap, job-lots of line, hooks, swivels, wire traces and any other expendable angling commodity can be on the one hand – if you are lucky – a good economical, value-for-money buy; but on the other, a sad, infuriating fiasco which can drive you to distraction if the item in question continually lets you down and loses you good fish which have taken a lot of time and expense to connect with.

Very few really first-class brands of dependable tackle ever get sold off cheaply at a mere fraction of their original full price cost, unless some most unusual happenings take place. At odd times, stock clearance sales do occur, or businesses are sold up quickly; then some really sound, value-for-money bargains are obtainable. However, my final sobering comment on the job-lot angling buy is: all very fine if you purchase a large quantity cheap and it suits you and performs well; but absolute disaster if you find yourself with a whole load of junky hooks or line in which you have not the slightest confidence. The safeguard when buying expendable items should be: start off with a small quantity and test it thoroughly; if

B

unreliable, consign it to the dustbin with an easy conscience – your financial loss has been negligible!

The lead casting weights used by beach, rock and pier fishermen are both many and varied and if you chance to live, and more important, fish in a 'tackle hungry', snaggy angling locality, where the shoreline is a mass of boulders or thick with kelp, you will most decidedly not be enamoured of buying the tackle shop variety, which are not too dear if you don't lose them, but hellishly expensive if you do, and by the dozen! To save shorecasters from continual financial embarrassment, the tackle trade very obligingly market a complete range of sinker moulds in all patterns and weights for the Do-It-Yourself exponent who can without difficulty lay his hands on a good supply of scrap lead. On this rather dangerous aspect of tackle making I will have much more to say in a later chapter on terminal tackles, with, I hasten to add, some very pointed remarks on the very necessary safety precautions which should always be taken when the handling of molten lead is being undertaken.

Depending on where you choose to fish and what sort of an angling temperament you have; will be the deciding factor as to whether you are a 'sitting' or 'standing' angler. My earliest memories of old-time shorecasters were: red-faced,

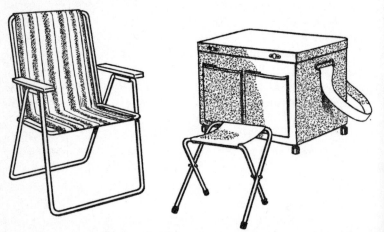

FIG. 1. Lightweight chair, stool and tackle-box seat

hoary-handed men in heavy rubber knee boots, old railway or police overcoats, their rods lashed with strong tanned cord (beachcombed from washed-up crab pots and long-lines) and high smelling 'fish basses'; who always stood, paced around, or crouched on their haunches with elbows on knees and hands clasped together. What those old stagers would have thought of our present-day range of shorecasters' furniture I have no idea, but, if like me you are well into middle age, and don't take too kindly to a seven- or eight-hour standing session, then the tackle catalogues can fit you up with the most luxurious lightweight chairs, combined tackle-boxes-cum-seats, and folding stools.

A very useful draught-beating piece of equipment which has filtered into the sea angling scene from the coarse fishers is the 'brolly'. In high winds or on very flat beaches, where the angler, is constantly moving position to follow the tide down and up, it is a nuisance. In calm weather however, especially at night, when the temperature drops very low; provided a fairly static fishing position is kept, a well pegged down umbrella of the biggest (45 in.) rib size will give an immeasurable amount of comfort and warmth, if a shallow pit or depression can be made and the umbrella erected over it at an angle, with the windward side 'shored-up' and sealed off with sand or shingle.

As the modern sea angler becomes more conservation minded, we find that instead of 'bashing everything on the head' that he catches and either eating it himself or if small, taking it home for the cat; he is becoming more selective and much to the amazement of the old school 'take 'em all' angler, keeps just one or two of his catch for the pot, and returns the rest, especially if he is an intelligent bass angler who wishes to preserve his future sport. From the coarse fishing scene – like the umbrella – has come the widespread use of the landing net as opposed to that 'finish 'em off' instrument the gaff, which I always associate with the heaving of conger eels or monster skate into boats.

While it is very skilful and satisfying – when the shore gently shelves – to play your fish to a standstill and then

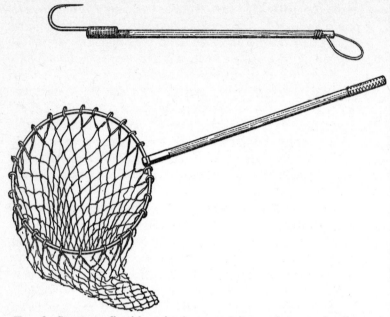

FIG. 2. Strong gaff with wrist loop, and heavy-duty sea landing net
with stout ash handle

wade in and beach it by hand (watching out for the tails of
thornbacks and the spines on bass), landing nets are a very
convenient solution to the knotty problem of safely securing
and bringing ashore large fish when you occupy a rocky ledge
with deep water beneath it. The three separate parts: handles,
frames and nets can all be bought as individual items, but
for saltwater fishing, plastic-covered steel frames and very
stout ash handles should be purchased; rather than the alloy
frames and light metal tubular, telescopic handles designed
for coarse fishing, which will not stand up to saltwater corrosion and the rough usage to which sea fishing gear is subjected. For the harbour wall and pier shorecaster, who is
fishing many feet above the water, a large, robust 'drop-net'
is the equivalent of life insurance. They are listed in the sea
angling section of your catalogues in various sizes, with a
long length of stout cord, to which should be tied a large

piece of cork as a safeguard against dropping 'your end' into the sea and having the whole lot sink out of sight before it can be retrieved by casting over it with your fishing tackle and getting it back again.

The greatest pitfall which faces the novice angler when he is buying his first set of shorecasting tackle is his own impetuosity. Instead of taking a very rational view of the whole subject and spending quite some time on the shoreline; talking, watching and summing up the situation and then drawing conclusions which guide him along the right path; he is apt, as soon as he can lay his hands on some available cash, to dash into a tackle shop, buy hastily, and then breathlessly proceed shorewards at a canter to discover to his eternal dismay (and the great amusement of all who are watching) just how unsuitable his rash, random purchases prove to be.

Sheer spending power can never be the answer to lack of knowledge. Some anglers have the most unhappy associations with every item of tackle they possess and are constantly searching – and paying out large amounts of cash – for what they imagine will be the perfect item, only to discard it or 'turn-it-in' for yet another piece of equipment which catches their eye. For the two basic items of the shorecasters' tackle – rod and reel – you can pay a very wide range of prices, starting at about £10 for each item and working up through the price range to the ultra-de-luxe models on which you could quite easily expend £100 for the two – gold plate and all!

Certain anglers accumulate masses of tackle, but very little 'shore-lore' and therefore catch very few fish; while other, less affluent souls who fish with the bare necessities – but the correct ones – and endlessly study their favourite patch of shore-line, are consistently successful in a quiet, unassuming manner which often escapes notice. One sure way to shorecasting resourcefulness, is to be forced, by circumstances to become a Do-It-Yourself tackle maker and bait provider. That way, you will certainly have to investigate thoroughly and understand all aspects of tackle design and methods of construction as well as put in some back-breaking time between the tidelines, following the sea in and out and discovering all kinds of things about shallow water marine creatures and the endless life cycle which they live, out on the littoral zone.

Top-priced, high-class shorecasting tackle is wonderful to own and fish with; it is, however, by no means absolutely essential for fish catching. It only succeeds in heightening the pleasure of it. As you thumb through your tackle catalogues and read in the angling press adverts all about the fascinating, but alas rather expensive world of fishing tackle, you may become despondent and wish you were a millionaire. Put such foolish thoughts aside and always try to bear in mind that a good angler can always eventually obtain some of the better class tackle; but a poor performer, even with the best gear, can never ever quite catch up on the experienced man, because such ability cannot be bought over the tackle shop counter. It is only gained the long, hard way, by spending many days and nights on the tideline in all weathers, constantly observing what is happening and fishing endlessly.

CHAPTER THREE

Rods

Although it is quite possible to take a walk along an angler-crowded beach, pier or rocky headland on a day when lots of fish are being caught and see all kinds of rods being used more or less successfully to do fish catching jobs for which they were not designed; when contemplating the purchase of a rod for shorecasting it is most satisfying to commence your fishing career with an item of tackle specifically made for the type of fishing you have in mind.

As the greater part of this book is concerned with shore-casting methods which demand the making of fairly long casts with the aid of lead weights of various sizes, a thorough understanding of the vital functions which rods for this fishing are called upon to perform, is important. First and foremost, such a beach or shorefishing rod is a casting tool. Its fish striking, playing and landing capabilities, whilst important, must always take a back, secondary seat, if it is to do correctly the job for which it is intended, and this aspect invariably leads to a rod being 'overpowered' fish-wise.

The most common example, I feel sure, is provided by the general purpose 12 ft. 'beachcaster' – universally known in angling parlance as a 'cod-pole'. This rod is designed to 'push-out' to around the 100-yard mark a weight (with baited hook included) of about 6 oz. when used in conjunction with a multiplier reel and line somewhere in the region of 20–30 lb. breaking strain. When considering the catch, shore caught cod, the majority of which will be under the four or five pound

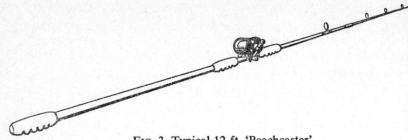

FIG. 3. Typical 12 ft. 'Beachcaster'

mark, with just one or two approaching and exceeding low double figures, such a powerful outfit seems completely un-justified in terms of 'fish taming' performance. However, if the angling venue where it is used is a stony beach with a strong lateral tide flow which really demands a 6 oz. wired 'grapple' lead to hold the terminal tackle in place, both the other items are necessary. The powerful rod to cast the weight effortlessly and the strong line to withstand the strain of cast-ing and 'breaking out the lead' when retrieving the tackle to rebait, or conversely, dislodge the lead and strike the hook home into a biting fish.

While it is the everlasting dream of all intelligent shore-casters to fish as light as possible and scale down their tackle so that the fish has the greatest possible chance to show its paces and swim unhampered on the end of a line free from weighty clutter; the strength of tidal flow, the nature of the ground over which the fishing is being done and the presence of line festooning weed, must always be given first considera-tion; otherwise the tackle used will be completely incapable of coping with the fishing conditions that prevail, and any fish hooked are most liable to be lost on the various snags when they are being reeled in.

To bring the utmost clarity into this discourse on shore-casting rods, it is first necessary to delve deeply into the various technical trade descriptions, advertising abbreviations and fisherman's jargon which quite often completely bewilder anyone who is seeking to become conversant with the subject.

The hollow glass rod blanks from which the better class of

'beachcasters' are constructed are described as having three distinct types of 'taper': standard; reverse and steep, when the rod specification is given. An immediate pointer to 'reverse' taper rods is the extra long length of butt piece which projects well down below the reel fitting and causes the angler using one of these rods to be severely handicapped by it when he is fishing a very rough, boulder-strewn beach. This butt section continually gets mixed up with his feet and on occasions trips him up so that he lands flat on his back with rod waving wildly! These reverse taper rods, where the blank not only tapers from the reel position up to the tip ring, but also has a reduction in thickness from the reel position down to the lower extremity of the butt section, have a very smooth and powerful casting action particularly suited to what is called the 'layback' style of casting, as they function with a 'bow' action. The top part bends back as it is compressed by the weight of the lead, and the lower section, also curving, produces a wonderfully controlled casting action when the rod reasserts or unwinds itself.

Standard taper rod blanks are almost always used for the cheaper solid glass beachcasters and those a little more expensive in hollow glass which have what are generally known as 'short handles', the butt of which comes somewhere in the region of the angler's lower midriff or groin, when they are in use. This type of rod is usually a foot or two shorter than the reverse taper type and is much more comfortable to use when rock fishing or on a rough shoreline because that hampering 'half a yard' down below is absent.

Steep taper blanks are a very recent innovation and when some of these beachcasting rods are viewed for the first time by shorecasters of long standing they are apt to be somewhat shocked by the very slender tips which such rods have, and be amazed when the rod performance specification blandly states: 'Suitable for casting weights between 2 and 9 oz.' The theory behind the design of these rods is that the greater the weight they are called upon to cast (within their weight-casting range of course), the greater the length of the rod which is brought into action. Also this rule applies when fish are being played and reeled in. I am of the opinion that their greatest asset lies in the amazingly sensitive tip section which certainly does register the slightest movement given by a fish mouthing or investigating the bait; but one drawback which all such slender-tipped rods have is that they do not take kindly to being used for what I will term 'rough-stuff' shore angling where lots of snagging is experienced and great bunches of tackle-straining weed have to be reeled in across a strong rush of tide.

One point on which I strongly disagree with certain tackle designers and manufacturers, is the recommended casting weight range which is accredited to some rods which more or less puts them into the 'perfect rod' category. To date there has never ever been such a thing. While some very reliable makers of high quality rods deem it necessary to design and produce three separate casting weight range types of rod, namely 1–3 oz. 3–6 oz. and 6–9 oz. and describe in detail the kinds of fishing to which each one is suited, a study of your catalogues will reveal rod specifications which candidly state in an unabashed style 'Will cast up to 12 oz. weights'.

It is a known fact that every beachcasting rod performs its very best casting action with just one ideal weight; like a car or motor-cycle with one certain cruising speed at which you can hear the engine is perfectly happy. A cod-pole of mine, which I made up myself from what the makers described as 1–8 oz. blanks, works wonderfully with a 5 oz. sinker. Above that, it feels as though it is straining. The action is heavy and the lead seems to be taxing the rod beyond its casting capabilities. Below that magical 5 oz. figure, the rod is performing at less than its optimum casting performance – there is just not enough weight in a 3 or 4 oz. sinker to give the best lead throwing performance.

When you finally go along to the tackle shop to buy a ready-made rod; or alternatively, reach the stage in making up a D.I.Y. rod kit where it can be assembled and the top ring whipped on, always wave it about for a few minutes and then, to really get the feel of it, hang on from the tip ring by a yard or so of nylon line (one after the other) an assortment of weights of various sizes and bounce them up and down a little to see exactly how the rod responds to them. Of course, the ideal way to purchase a rod is to take a whole armful of them out on to a secluded casting court, a lonely beach or a deserted playing field and try each one out individually with varying sizes of weights until you are able to make a leisurely choice of the one which suits you the best. This is the stage in your tackle selecting which will benefit from all the 'shore-chatting' and 'angler-watching' experiences which I suggested you should have before you take the irrevocable step of part-ing with your cash for fishing gear which you fervently hope will be suitable and catch you lots of fish!

As the designers and manufacturers of rod blanks become steadily more efficient and successful at their task, they de-mand ever-increasing lightness, strength and durability in the fittings which are to grace their treasured brain-children, the 'Super-special-high-density-fast-taper-thin-walled' hollow glass rod members. Heavy rods, which are intended to be rested in either monopods, or on tripods, and used for general beach fishing where the angler expects just the one rod to serve a multitude of purposes; are usually fitted by the manufacturers – quite sensibly – with fittings which are appropriately robust. A heavy, chrome-on-brass, screw-lock reel fitting is standard equipment. So also are reinforced ferrules and large, steel framed ceramic lined rings, usually of 'Regalox' which is a vitrified, high-alumina ceramic, having a hardness somewhere between that of sapphire and diamond, with a pinkish appear-ance and a complete resistance to salt water.

To put such fittings as those described on a 'thoroughbred' set of lightweight blanks, designed to cast 1–3 oz. weights and intended to be made up into a hand-held bass rod, would be piscatorial sacrilege. No doubt the blank maker would have already solved the buyer's ferrule problem by putting his extra special product on to the market with the latest 'Spigot' ferrule already incorporated. The spigot ferrule is a new in-novation which dispenses with the metal tube male and female fittings which were glued, pinned or heated and shrunk on to

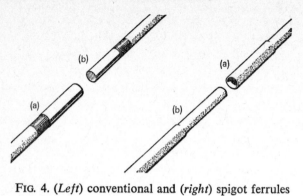

FIG. 4. (*Left*) conventional and (*right*) spigot ferrules

the butt and top rod joints. Simply and briefly explained a hollow or solid glass spigot or plug is glued to project from the top of the lower rod blank where the traditional female ferrule would normally be placed, and the bottom end of the top joint of the rod fits *over* it like a sleeve.

The advantages of spigot ferrules are: lightness, absence of the stiffening effect which metal ferrules give to the two heavily-reinforced joined rod sections, and a refreshing freedom from 'ferrule-stick', which has caused many anglers of my acquaintance and myself to struggle frantically at packing-up time, sometimes in a howling gale with torrential rain, to heave apart the butt and top sections of a beachcaster, the ferrules of which have become inexplicably locked in a tight, loving embrace!

At the present time 'bare-pole' rods are all the rage, especially among the lightweight tackle brigade who have dispensed with all but the most essential fittings on their D.I.Y. creations. With the advent of ultra-light rod blanks incorporating spigot ferrules, a great movement for dispensing with all unnecessary encumbrances on rods was started, and the forerunners of this trend first cast their eyes upon those outlandish, enormous rubber buttons, the great long cork handles and the clumsy, thick brass screw winch fittings; accoutrements beloved of the 'stick-in-the-mud' traditionalist rod-makers of the old school. The lot was abandoned, butt-buttons, corks and ton-heavy reel retainers. After careful thought, the mere idea of a permanently placed reel fitting was forgotten! Since the makers of most good multipliers provided a rod clamp with long bolts and two wing nuts; why bother with a reel fitting? What could be easier than to encase the bottom three feet of the rod blank in shrink-on non-slip P.V.C. sleeving and then clamp on the reel to the rod butt in any desired position which facilitates easy casting, sandwiching a piece of thin foam rubber between the rod clamp and the sleeving to prevent it from becoming damaged and torn.

Having solved quite easily and weightlessly the rod handle covering and reel seating problem, all that remained was the whipping on of a set of really featherweight rod rings so that the very delicate action of the specially designed rod blank would not be thrown off balance or impaired by lots of heavily armoured rod rings which added unwanted weight in the tip region. The avoidance of extra weight here was particularly important if the tip velocity was not to be slowed down and the casting performance ruined.

Such a rod as the one I have just described cannot generally be found in the tackle shops, especially if it has been made up from a drab-green set of rod blanks which have been purposely left unvarnished or proofed (they really don't need all that 'glass-coated' finish you know). In addition, if the 'Harchrome' rings have been sensibly whipped on to the rod with nylon monofil in the 15 lb. breaking-strain range, there is absolutely no reason why the whippings should be proofed or treated. It is a well-known, and lamentable, fact among anglers (and the makers and sellers of fishing tackle if they are truthful) that certain items of gear catch more anglers than they do fish. Gaily painted floats are irresistible to coarse fishermen, no matter how useless or bad their design. Likewise most anglers, except a very few out-and-out fanatics, are completely taken in by a tremendous amount of 'flash' on a fishing rod. Chrome fittings, bright red or even jazzy striped whippings, gleaming gold and silver labels halfway up the butt section and the whole of the varnished sections gleaming with a mirror-like fish-scaring gloss.

All this window-dressing or rod-rack appeal which really does nothing for the rod so far as fish catching ability is concerned, unfortunately, in these times of astronomical labour costs, has to be paid for very dearly by the angler. Small wonder that the army of D.I.Y. tackle makers, especially in the field of tailored-to-taste fishing rods is on the increase.

Money-saving Methods

To depart from the joyous subject of fishing and talk about such painfully mundane subjects as relative costs for a paragraph or two. Let me make a few money-saving comparisons which I trust will prove most enlightening to those whose financial resources are in no way comparable with their enthusiasm for shorecasting – which is limitless!

For the benefit of those indolent or ham-fisted souls, who have either no desire to make tackle or are unable to even sharpen a pencil without disembowelling themselves; let me recommend the very wide open field of the second-hand, or to dress it up nicely, like the tackle dealers do, 'part-used' market. According to the present fashion of the day in rods, those which have been in use and on the market for some time seem to lose popularity and suffer a sudden inexplicable fall in price somewhere about their fourth, or at the most, fifth anniversary. It is not that they are obsolete, or no longer efficient for the job they used to perform; usually they are killed stone dead in their infancy by the sheer 'gimmickry' of other rods which appear and are in great demand by almost everyone literally overnight!

This is the wide-open field of rod buying into which the 'beginner' shorecaster can step and avail himself of some wonderful bargains if he is able to plonk down upon the tackle shop counter instant cash. A bundle of notes ready in the hand will enable some of the hardest bargains imaginable to be driven as no tackle dealer worth his salt likes to see an angler's money replaced in his pocket because a fair price could not be agreed upon. Generally speaking, second-hand gear, in very good condition, unless it is really old, fetches on the open tackle market a price somewhere in the region of half to two-thirds of its new price. Due to taxation, immediately a new rod is purchased and taken from the shop its value falls alarmingly and it can usually only be 'turned-in' again to the tackle dealer for about half its purchase price, if you intend buying other goods the price of which is well in excess of the amount he is allowing you for the second-hand stuff.

Owing to the fact that a tackle dealer must make a profit to cover his expenses when re-selling second-hand gear, as he is seldom in the business for the good of his health or to be a guardian angel to anglers, an amateur in the market for tackle can give a better price to someone afflicted with the 'chop-and-change' tackle-swapping mania than he would get by going to a dealer for a part-exchange allowance. The vital secret of second-hand tackle buying is a complete finger-tip knowledge of every item of tackle which is available for that particular branch of the sport in which you are interested, and the instant ability to put on it a mental price-tag which is somewhere near the price which it would be offered by a tackle dealer.

According to your finances, you must equip yourself with a set of tackle which is all more or less in the same price range, otherwise you will overspend on certain items and then be forced by monetary circumstances to be skimpy on the price of other articles, and finish up with a selection of very high- and also embarrassingly low-grade tackle, the cheapest items of which may let you down lamentably when you are in the very act of taking some good fish.

It is an undisputable fact that all discerning anglers who take their sport seriously, eventually reach the state of efficiency when they come to the conclusion that shop-finished rods have no longer the personal requirements that D.I.Y. ones have. In angling, I am happy to report that this trend is in no way stifled or frowned upon by the tackle manufacturers and dealers. Just the reverse, it is nurtured and pandered to, because the tackle trade knows that if they do not willingly supply all the angler's requirements, some other astute person who deals in another commodity will instantly realise that there is an opening for him, and jump in to fill the gap by selling the increasing army of nimble-fingered fishermen just what they require.

Speaking in terms of sheer hard cash, a D.I.Y. rod can be made up from a 'kit' for just about half the 'finished' over-the-counter shop price. Put another way. If you have allocated about £20 for a rod and reel, you could perhaps get a rod of the kind you require for all of that amount at the new made-up price, but certainly not a reel as well. But a £10 D.I.Y. kit would make up into a 'finished' £20 value rod, leaving £10 for the reel of your choice.

Of course, without a shadow of a doubt, the greatest advantage of D.I.Y. rod making (cash considerations apart) is the absolute personal tailored-to-taste details you can incorporate. Short, slightly built anglers (under 5 ft. 6 in. tall and weighing about 10 stones) do not usually perform well or comfortably with long, heavy rods, and it is a lamentable fact that practically all beachcasters are made for 'fourteen-stoners' who are beefy and 6 ft. tall in their stockinged feet! One vital consideration which should be decided carefully by the angler who is to use the rod, is the distance from the extremity of the butt to the reel position. This should be adjustable in a shop bought 'made-up' rod, as individual arm lengths differ greatly and these are in some cases completely unrelated to the height of the person or his body frame size. You will find that quite a number of shop rods have their reel fittings fixed permanently at a distance to suit an angler with a 30 in. reach – armpit to extended finger tips – and this is most uncomfortable for a short-armed angler. This one factor alone is sufficient cause for making a D.I.Y. rod, as it is of paramount importance to a smooth, backlash free casting technique when a multiplier reel is being used.

Quite a stir is being made in present day beachcasting circles by certain way-out items of tackle which have infiltrated into the fringe of general angling use from the 'Tournament Surfcasting' world in which the prime consideration is distance of cast. The ultra-fast taper, stiff butted (a length of dural tube fused into the hollow glass butt section) 'tournament' style rod is all the rage just now; but its effectiveness and suitability for general shorecasting is being seriously questioned by some sea anglers and applauded by others. So we have a rift in our ranks. And from my circumspect survey of the whole situation, I am apt to form the opinion that too much 'distance mania' and not enough 'common-sense angling technique' is a retrograde step which can lead to endless frustrations so far as the catching of fish is concerned, and that observation is particularly pertinent to shorecasting beginners.

So far, when considering rods for shorecasting, the accent has been heavily on stoutish poles to be used with leads around the 4–8 oz. mark and strong lines in a breaking-strain range of 15–35 lb. Generally, this is the tackle most suitable for locations where there is a strong to medium tidal flow and distance casting with a lead weight is the accepted method of getting the bait out to the fish. However, beachcasters or surf-fishing rods are by no means the only ones which are employed for certain angling locations where the conditions are vastly different. The coarse fishers' pike and carp rods are eminently suitable for some types of shore fishing, particularly where light leads of 1 or 2 oz. need to be cast accurately with lines of up to 10 lb. b.s. used in conjunction with a fixed-spool or small multiplier reel. Also, some coarse-fishing rods, around the 10, 11 and 12 ft. mark, which have been designed specifically for legering for barbel and chub in rivers, make first class sea angling float- and bottom-fishing rods when used with fixed-spool or centre-pin reels and lines in the 5 or 6 lb. range, and suitably balanced terminal tackle.

In the quiet waters of harbours, tidal lagoons and estuaries (where the fishing may not always be free) the lightest of coarse fishing match tackle is often necessary to take the various, often very wily and shy, sea fish species which frequent such locations. The mullet especially, which are often reputed to be completely uncatchable until some very resourceful angler who is an all-rounder comes along and instead of pursuing them with the long-accepted methods and gear, with great ingenuity, adapts coarse fishing methods and tackle (and perhaps, by fishing for them with floating crust or cheese paste, in the traditional 'chub' or 'carp' style) proceeds completely to outwit them and bring quite a number to his landing net.

With a little adaptation and lots of common sense, I find, that in addition to the shorecasting rods I possess, I can on the right occasions, use to very good effect all my coarse fishing gear as well!

CHAPTER FOUR

Reels

Although, in the previous chapter, we thoroughly investigated the various rods which can be used for shorecasting, basically they are all the same in their construction and appearance. Shorecasting reels however, which you will see in use along the harbour walls, piers, beaches and rocky foreshores, will fall into three different categories which are widely dissimilar in appearance and performance. The selection of the one which you prefer and will be happy with is quite a serious business.

Immediately anyone starts to become interested in shore-casting and begins to weigh up the tackle aspects of it, they will find that the field, where reels are concerned, is very sharply divided – and never in twain shall both sides agree. The multiplier men in all their long-distance casting glory on the one hand, and the fixed-spool exponents on the other, staunchly supporting their choice of gear and advising beginners to start with their type of reel as it will give instant casting ability without practice, and not the slightest fear of an over-run and a blistered thumb to prove it!

Somewhere in the middle – between these two schools of thought in reel design and efficiency – stands a very small gathering of the other, third reel types; the Scarborough, centre-pin, or side-cast users. And strange to relate, most of these anglers swear by their kind of reel and denounce the multiplier and fixed-spool addicts as new-fangled gadgeteers of the worst possible kind. What a bewildering business, and how off-putting on first appearance for the angling beginner to come to terms with himself and decide upon a reel!

To make the reel conundrum even more complicated and frustrating, some tackle dealers, instead of remaining completely impartial and open-minded towards their clients' free-agency so far as choice is concerned, try by devious means to inveigle their customers into buying what they themselves prefer and use. And if, unfortunately, they are of the anti-multiplier brigade who are prone to scoff at the very idea of an angler taking his new tackle out on to a secluded field for a few practice casting sessions before he makes his debut on the shore, the beginner will be sent off happily shorewards with a 'sea-size' fixed-spool reel, secure in the knowledge that he can commence his fishing immediately without the slightest fear of a lash-up.

Over the years, I have given this fixed-spool versus multiplier controversy some serious thought, and after observing quite a number of anglers making their initial purchases, and listening in to the tackle shop talk that took place, I have come to some revealing conclusions regarding the psychological side of it which I shall now impart to guide my readers along the right lines and give them an insight into the quandary which faces a tackle dealer who wishes to preserve a good customer-dealer relationship.

On many more occasions than I would care to number, I have witnessed a dejected angler standing all deflated before a highly sympathetic tackle dealer, with an almost new multiplier reel on the counter between them, full of snarled-up 'over-run' line. A scene of the utmost sadness – and the conversations go something like this. Greenhorn angler: 'I find it absolutely impossible to get on with this reel. I've read the booklet and done all you told me – but look what has happened! That is the third new lot of line I've had on it this week. Please can I turn it in for a fixed-spool, the same kind as Joe Bloggs is using. He advised me to get rid of this multiplier and change over to something less complicated.'

Is there any wonder that, after a tackle dealer has had that poignant little episode repeated in his shop at least once a week for years, he takes the easy way out and recommends fixed-spool reels to beginners, and relies on a steady sale of multipliers to other experienced 'shore-bashers' who have surmounted all the pitfalls and can use them faultlessly? By this means, he keeps the peace, preserves some beautiful friendships, and does not have a second-hand shelf full of slightly-used multipliers tying up his capital and gathering dust.

Yet another slant on this baffling multiplier or fixed-spool controversy, is the left- or right-hand wind mystery, which to this day I have failed to resolve. Get out your tackle catalogues, angling magazines or trade 'blurb' leaflets and look first at all the fixed-spool reels shown. I'll guarantee they all have a left-hand wind. Now switch to the multiplier reel photographs or illustrations and you will discover that they are all shown as having right-hand winds. Somewhere along the line (again pardon my angling-flavoured pun) there must be a connection. Do all the prospective right-handed anglers choose multipliers and all the left-handed ones fixed-spool reels? To add to this puzzling situation, there are quite a lot of right-hand wind fixed-spool reels on the market and some on which the winding handle is interchangeable – but strange as it may appear, very few firms manufacturing multiplier reels make one in a left-hand wind.

A rare group of anglers I have not yet mentioned are the dual-reel exponents, who use both multipliers and fixed-spool reels and seem ill-at-ease with either. Their theory is that while it is reasonably easy to operate a multiplier reel in daylight and make fairly long trouble-free casts, when darkness falls the 'gremlins' appear and it is wiser to change over to a fixed-spool reel than risk an ego-destroying over-run which seems to unsettle your concentration for the rest of the angling session.

So far, very little has been said about the minority group who are centre-pin, Scarborough, or side-cast fanatics. There is a saying along the East Yorkshire coast which I am sure is well founded and true. It is that you must have grown up with a Scarborough reel, otherwise you would never willingly try using one in preference to another kind which is far less fearsome if you make a mistake with it.

Now let us delve very deeply into the performance, design, advantages, drawbacks, price and' peculiarities of the three separate types of reel under consideration, so that a working knowledge of each is clearly imprinted upon your mind's eye. Thus you will be adequately equipped with the know-how which is vital to successful reel buying.

The Multiplier Reel

The multiplier, as its name implies, is a geared, revolving drummed reel, the majority of which retrieve line in a ratio of about 3:1. This means that for every complete revolution of the winding handle the drum revolves three times. Certain expensive, automatic gear-change models have a retrieve of about $2\frac{1}{2}:1$ and $4\frac{1}{2}:1$. The ratio depends on whether you are just reeling in your terminal tackle, which would come in fast at $4\frac{1}{2}:1$, or a large, powerful fish fighting your reel handle all the way and making winding-in difficult, when the reel would 'think' for you and drop down into low-gear or a $2\frac{1}{2}:1$ ratio.

A very careful examination of the multipliers listed in your tackle catalogues will reveal that the larger, heavier models with metal spools are recommended and designed for boat fishing, and the lighter, smaller models, often with two plastic or unbreakable glass-filled nylon spools, are intended for shorecasting. This point must be uppermost in your mind if you are buying a second-hand reel, otherwise you could find yourself attempting to cast with a very rugged, heavyweight metal-spooled boat reel. The drum would probably develop so much inertia when you cast with it, that it would remove quite an amount of skin from your thumb, and perhaps flesh as well, if you tried to brake it in the accepted shorecasting manner.

The most serious drawback of the multiplier reel is the tendency to back-lash or over-run. Various devices and much effort has been devoted towards producing a reel which is entirely free of this effect. Centrifugal governors, adjustable

spool tensioners, oil 'drag' retarders, and of late, exterior 'lift
and brake' gadgets, have all been incorporated into, or clipped
and screwed on to, shorecasting multiplier reels to assist in
eliminating this infuriating and confidence-destroying effect.

It is safe to say, I am sure, that most of them are quite
effective because not only do they iron-out to a certain degree
the casting irregularities of the angler using them, but in
addition they provide him with that much needed confidence
to purchase and attempt to use a multiplier reel, rather than
duck the issue altogether and with a faint heart, settle at the
outset for the easily used, and mastered (though far less
efficient for certain kinds of angling) fixed-spool reel.

Although it is possible to cast in an erratic, uncontrolled,
jerky manner with a fixed-spool reel, and if the line is strong
enough, continue to do so without suffering the consequences
of a permanently faulty casting style. No matter what kind of
automatic cast-smoothing, braking devices are fitted to a
multiplier reel, there is always the danger that if a thoroughly
bad snatching style is performed, it will produce the in-
evitable snarl-up and break-off. I firmly believe that such
unfortunate happenings do much to chasten the careless
shorecaster who lacks co-ordination and concentration, and
eventually produce better results from him so far as casting
technique is concerned, if he takes heed and strives to rectify
his errors.

Multiplier reels need 'mothering' more than any other item
of fishing tackle, and if you are not prepared to give them
immediate attention each time they are brought home from
a fishing session, then it is wise to steer clear of the expense
incurred in buying one and settle for some other reel which
does not demand such a high initial cash outlay or a devoted
cleaning ritual. If you take as true the sweeping statements
to be seen in tackle advertisements, and really do leave your
treasured multiplier reel in your fishing bag after an outing to
'Shrug off the sand and saltwater', please don't be horrified
at the condition of it a month later when you chance to give
it a cursory inspection!

Sand, windblown grit and dust, and that devilish archenemy of the shoreline, saltwater spray, rapidly play absolute havoc with all fishing gear if it is not properly cleaned and maintained after each outing. This is a job which has to be faced, and no amount of oil, grease or aerosol 'proof-sprays' will obviate the need for constant cleaning, rinsing in fresh water, and frequent inspections to make sure no pockets of salt-laden moisture are carrying out a deadly eroding effect on any metal parts, no matter how heavily chromium-plated they are and supposedly immune to such attacks.

A long time ago, when I was young and foolish, I once bedded down for the summer an expensive, treasured multiplier reel in oily rags and a plastic bag, after cleaning all the metal parts meticulously by doing a complete strip-down of all the works and then re-assembling it. Unfortunately, I completely overlooked the line on the spool which had been reeled in on the last outing and not run off, rinsed in fresh water, and dried before being re-loaded. Tucked safely away in its warm airing cupboard, the deadly salt water, which dried out from the line, deposited salt crystals on all the metal parts, where they ate deeply into the 'salt-proof' chrome like hungry termites! Imagine my dismay when I unwrapped the reel to check it for the winter cod season and found it suffering from a bad attack of saltwater 'small-pox' – all the metal parts were deeply pitted and crumbling away in a greyish-black dust! The moral for tackle preservation: lots of rinsing in fresh warm water until all the sea water is removed, a thorough drying, and then on with a liberal coating of grease. Do not forget to remove the line on reels if you store them away for any length of time.

The Fixed-spool Reel

Let us now consider the fixed-spool reel, its limitations and the types of fishing to which it is best suited. First of all, let me fearlessly declare, despite what the makers claim to the contrary, that by its design and the way in which the line is spooled by the bale arm, this reel is in no way suited to the heaviest kinds of shorecasting. One of the greatest faults in its performance is the lack of 'direct-pull' line retrieve and the fact that the line turns through an angle of 90° before it is pushed by the bale arm on to the end-on mounted spool.

When fishing over very snaggy ground with a powerfully actioned rod and very strong line – say in the 30 lb. breaking strain range – whenever a snag is hit with the terminal tackle, the whole of the pull is concentrated upon the bale arm and because it does not have direct winching on to a revolving spool, a great deal of winding power seems to be lost in transmission from the cranking handle, through the gears to the actual winding-in part which is the side-push bale arm.

With lines of up to the 10 lb. breaking strain and a light-actioned rod designed to cast weights around 1 or 2 oz. the fixed-spool reel reigns supreme. Used wisely for the lightest of shorecasting with lead weights and bait, and also for spinning, it is unbeatable because a very light lure or set of baited terminal tackle can be cast with it over long distances with the greatest accuracy. This is the field in which the coarse fishermen use it to good effect, but when the larger, saltwater models are tested to see how they compare in performance with multiplier reels, the following three drawbacks will be found.

First: a fixed-spool reel of coarse fishing size designed to perform with a light line will cast long distances with ease if the spool is correctly loaded so that the line comes to within an eighth of an inch of the spool lip. However, a 'sea-size' reel of that type, loaded with 25–30 lb. nylon will soon lose its casting advantage because once the first fifty or sixty yards of this thicker, heavier line has run off the spool, a deep well is created and the rest of the line, to complete the cast, has to jump up over the spool lip an ever-increasing distance as the spool empties.

Secondly: large fixed-spool reels loaded with strong lines and used in conjunction with heavy weights are unnerving to cast as they develop a great deal of 'line-lash' around the uppermost casting hand of the angler, whose wrist and the fingers holding the rod are immediately in the line of fire. A friend of mine, before he changed over to a multiplier reel for shorecasting, always wore a long, thick leather gauntlet glove on his above-the-reel hand for protection, because he suffered from an abiding fear that one day, at the commencement of a really beefy cast, a loop of line would suddenly snarl up around his fingers and take a few of them right off!

Finally: the age-old, ever-present bogey of line twist or kinking, which has been a major drawback ever since the fixed-spool reel, with its slipping-clutch mechanism which could be set to let the spool slip just as the breaking strain of the line is reached, was invented. This aspect of the reel's performance is a boon if used wisely in the correct manner. Unfortunately, in very heavy sea fishing, certain situations arise where the tackle is suddenly subjected to great strain. On these occasions (a great bunch of weed on the line, a very large fish almost beached but still struggling in a heavy surf, or a fish being reeled in when the trailing lead is suddenly snagged and comes to a halt on the bottom) that a dangerous mistake can be made. The reel is cranked furiously with the handle by an excited angler at the same instant that the slipping clutch is releasing line to prevent a breakage. Although it is not always apparent to anglers, because I see them constantly doing this 'winding-in' business when the audable click-click line release warning is operating, what is actually happening to the line is that the bale arm is revolving and attempting to deposit line upon the spool, but at the same time the tension pulling the line off is so great that the spool is slipping and line is coming off while the revolving of the bale arm is causing it to be released with a twist. If not too many kinks have been put into the line it may lay upon the spool in quite neat coils. However, watch out for squalls the next time a long, smooth cast is attempted. The twisted line may spring off the spool in tight coils and instead of being smoothed out and released by the large butt ring, which is usually fitted to rods for use with fixed-spool reels, it builds up into a formidable bird's nest which may even decide the fixed-spool devotee to consider seriously the idea of turning it in *for a multiplier* ... which would completely baffle the tackle dealer!

The Scarborough Reel

To round up the reel controversy, let us now take a close look at the minority group of reel users: the Scarborough and side-cast reel exponents. In direct variance with what I have said about maintenance so far as multiplier and fixed-spool reels are concerned, to prevent rapid deterioration by the effects of salt deposits, I know Yorkshire rock anglers who quite cheerfully and without the slightest qualm, leave their turned-walnut-and-brass Scarborough reels on their rods in the corner of an outhouse from one year's end to the next without the slightest attention other than an occasional squirt of oil into the ball races, or brass-bush and spindle, just to keep it free running. Such items of fishing tackle are often handed down from generation to generation, father to son, and the knowledge and knack of how to cast with them seems to be hereditary also!

There are two schools of thought in Scarborough reel usage: the clock-wise and the anti-clockwise back winders. With the back-wind, the line flows in straight through the rod rings and on to the reel spool giving a direct wind, whereas the ordinary popular clock-wise wind brings the line down, away from the rod butt after it leaves the bottom rod ring. I must admit – having tried both ways – that it seems very unnatural to wind in backwards; but it is in the technique of casting where the anti-clock wind shows its advantage. By having the line flow from the reel parallel to, and very near to, the rod butt, a great deal of friction against the butt ring is prevented and this appreciably aids the making of long, smooth casts. Also the line can be held by the forefinger of the uppermost hand and trapped against the rod, where it is held secure during the build-up of the 'start with your back to the water' side-swipe cast, which is a traditional characteristic of the famous Scarborough style.

The Side-cast Reel

A reel which combines the direct-pull, powerful winching effect of the simple Scarborough reel with the casting line released of the fixed-spool reel, is the side-cast. In addition, it also has the very desirable refinements of an adjustable 'star-drag' and an audible ratchet or check which makes it particularly suitable for taking large fish from the shore. The biggest models are very strongly made (although rather large and heavy) and are designed to hold something like 300 yards of 30 lb. line, or alternatively around 600 yards of 15 lb. b.s. line.

Unlike the drum of the Scarborough reel, the side-cast 'line-well' is quite shallow and tapers up towards the winding handle side so that when the reel is swung on its special mounting, to turn sideways on to the rod in its casting position, the line spills quite freely over the spool lip. This is one reel which can be used for very heavy boat angling as well as shorecasting and this point should be noted by anyone who wishes to take the minimum of tackle on a fishing holiday, where a mixture of heavy bottom fishing from a boat, as well as shorecasting, is to be done.

Buying your Reel

Before I put on my judge's wig and start my summing-up of shorecasting reels from the evidence I have set before you, let me attempt to put prospective reel buyers – both new and second-hand-on the right track so far as the purchasing of reliable reels, with good sound after-sales service is concerned. Except for the all-important reel; there is really very little which can go wrong with the other items of your shorecasting tackle which can bring your fishing to an abrupt and permanent halt. Apart from really bad accidents, like standing on the top of your rod and shattering it, having a truly enormous fish run off the whole of your line and then snap it at the spool knot, or forgetting that your Tilley lamp is perched precariously on a rock and having it knocked off with a sudden gust of wind on a pitch black night, which plunges you suddenly into 'power-cut' gloom, very little else can put a stop to your fishing, except a faulty reel. Before some wiseacre chirps up and tells me glibly that all good anglers should carry a spare one, I would advise him to turn to the book cover, read the title again, and then find me on any beach half a dozen shorecasting *beginners* who are of sufficient affluence to carry a spare reel, just in case!

So, it really is important to buy a most reliable reel from a tackle dealer who can cure its minor troubles from his stock of spares immediately, or return it to the agents or makers (most decidedly not abroad) from whence it returns, as new in one week – for certain! The first precaution anyone should take when buying a second-hand reel, is to make absolutely sure, before he even puts a finger on it, that it is not an obsolete model which is out of production. Failure to do this may result in a sad little insertion in the 'Wants' column of an angling newspaper which reads: 'Wanted for spares Slick-Cast mark 4 – Urgent.'

If you purchase new, or make up a D.I.Y. rod, you will surely take great pains to put on the reel fitting where it suits you. This means that you must decide which type of reel you are going to fish with and buy one so that it can be attached to the rod temporarily and a few casts made to ensure everything is just right. Of course, a second-hand rod and reel brought as one job-lot presents quite a few problems, such as, does the reel suit?, is the fitting in a position to match the buyer's arm-reach?, and how is the rod for length and weight so far as its new owner's height and physique are concerned?

Should you have the great good fortune to be blessed with an angling friend who is a thoroughly experienced shore-fisher and who will allow you to try your hand at casting with a variety of reels, then I feel certain you will be able to shortcut and quite easily surmount this very knotty final choice of a reel. What you must avoid at all costs is everlastingly to take the easy way out and plump for items of tackle which are primarily designed to please faint hearted who are so gullible that they are willing to sacrifice efficiency for ease of use.

Some aspiring shorecasters, who I am quite sure have a wrong psychological approach to angling; demand, and try to buy for cash over the tackle shop counter what I will call 'Instant Fishing'. After parting with their money, they are quite convinced that they should immediately be able to make for the tideline and perform in a highly efficient manner – otherwise the tackle is to blame! These poor, misguided souls demand that their angling shall be one hundred per cent pleasure, with no irksome practise or mental concentration involved in any shape or form. To develop a highly skilled shorecasting technique is a very difficult, but exceedingly worthwhile accomplishment, once it has been attained. To anyone whose sole aim in angling is to sacrifice skill for ease of operation let me recommend not a rod and line, but a trawl. That way the engine on the boat can be made to do all the donkey work . . . and what is more the catch is bigger!

CHAPTER FIVE

Monopods, Tripods, Lines and Terminal Tackles

Although quite a number of very accomplished shorecasters whom I have observed fishing with ultra-light, hand-held tackle have dispensed with rod rests or holders altogether and tuck the rod under their arm when baiting up or unhooking a fish; I do not recommend this procedure to beginners. They will invariably make the fatal error of dropping the whole outfit with a sickening clang on to the rocks or worse still, into the sand! A good rod and precision multiplier reel does not take kindly to such careless treatment; on rocks the rather brittle steel rod rings are liable to shatter; the reel cage will often be knocked out of true and the handle become bent. Sand, although it softens the fall, plays havoc with the 'innards' of the reel the next time a cast is made, unless the whole thing is taken apart and thoroughly rinsed in lots of fresh water. To obviate such infuriating, time-wasting and often rather expensive accidents, well designed, reliable rod retaining equipment is of paramount importance. Sad to relate, exactly what is required cannot always be purchased, so a D.I.Y. attitude to this essential item is often the best.

The Monopod

Monopods, or one-legged 'spike' rod rests, are intended for use on sand, hard-packed shingle, mud, or a firm mixture of sand and large or small stones. One drawback to the shop-bought variety is that they have either no footrest with which they can be driven into 'the hard stuff' or such a small, inadequate one, that your foot either slips off, or you wear a hole in the sole of your boot while trying to stamp the rest in. Beware of, and avoid like the plague, any monopod you may see which has a foot 'driving' rest which is merely a triangular piece of metal welded to the stem. Such things are lethal, especially if not well rounded off or turned over to get rid of sharp corners. One unfortunate angler of my acquaintance, whilst attempting to drive such a badly finished rest into hard-packed shingle in the dark, let his wet, muddy boot instep slip off it and the sharp metal footrest sliced right through his thick rubber boot and gouged a sizeable chunk out of his ankle!

The main trouble with monopods which come ready-made from tackle shops is that they have a number of very common faults which are not immediately apparent until they have been bought and put into use. Taking into consideration the angler's height and the length of the rod butt below the reel mounting, the monopod should, when pushed firmly into the beach, hold the rod in a position which allows the user to rush up and grab it easily at the correct place for striking and reeling in. Too low down and he will have to stoop to get the rod out, too high up and he will have to almost shin up the rod rest to extract the rod and get into his action stance.

It is essential that you are able to operate a well designed monopod with just one hand and foot, because if you have to grasp it with both hands to drive it into difficult ground (perhaps it has no footrest) what do you do with your rod while you are carrying out this double-handed planting procedure? A final snag which I have experienced with monopods which were obviously designed by angling theorists instead of experienced beach-bashers: one-legged rod-rests must have a stabilising fin or horizontal bar-cum-footrest which can be pushed firmly below the sand or gravel level to lock them into position. Some beautifully finished shop-bought beach sticks have just a very sharp, slender spike which drives in with glorious ease; but watch out ... The moment you place your rod in them and turn your back to extract something from your tackle bag, they swing round seawards with the pull of the tide on your line, and your rod slips out of the 'U' groove and topples over into the surf or on to the beach.

The best tailor-made monopods I have ever seen are those which a friend of mine creates from genuine ex-Railway hickory and mild steel shunting poles. First the wiggly pig's-tail metal hook is heated up in a fire and hammered out straight. The next step is to stick the pole into the lawn and measure up the rod to it to get the position for the bottom rod butt cup and the 'U' shaped retainer. Take into consideration, of course, the height of the angler (who preferably should be making up the rod rest), which ensures that the height of the rested rod is right for his hands to grab it quickly in the correct fishing position. With the surplus handle part of the pole sawn off, the bottom rod butt cup screwed into position and the 'U' shaped retainer fixed on near the top, these shunting-pole rod rests are wonderfully stable and can be quite easily pushed right down into the most difficult ground with one hand.

For really heavy-duty 'rough-stuff' monopods, a suitable length of thick 1 in. diameter mild steel tube takes some beating. Flatten one end and point it off. Weld very securely a 6 in. footrest of the same material to the upright about 12 in. from the bottom point in a horizontal position and then after planting it in the lawn and measuring yourself and the

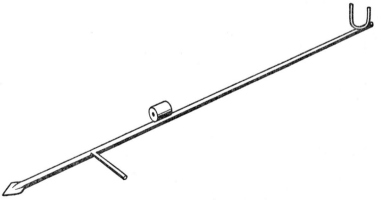

FIG. 5. A 'rough-stuff' monopod

C

rod against it, weld the metal butt cup and the 'V' or 'U' shaped retainer into position in their appropriate places. A rod rest such as this is almost indestructible. Although it is rather heavy to carry long distances, you most certainly can drive it into the roughest beach by standing heavily on the footrest and swinging the top round in small circles with the hand which is not holding your rod.

Incidentally, a good strong monopod makes a wonderful cliff climbing stick, ground tester, and step digger, if you are like me and walk long distances to find suitable gullies and holes, and then have to scramble up and down over some very rough terrain in the dark to fish them.

The Tripod

Tripods (and occasionally two-legged bipods) seem to be far more popular with shorecasters than the single-spiked monopods, mainly I think because the occasions on which a tripod must be used are far more numerous. Concrete or stone piers where there are no traditional guard-rails for the angler to lean his rod against call for the use of a firm, adjustable support. I have on occasions seen some thoughtless anglers damaging the wooden pier decking or jetty edging of fishing stations by driving in a very sharp pointed monopod; and be warned, that kind of irresponsibility can only lead to either being ordered off by the property owners or piermaster and perhaps banned from ever using such a vantage point for angling again.

Rock fishers most certainly need a strong rod support and I have found metal tripods with long adjustable legs and a 'bag-hook' beneath the head-piece to be particularly effective. It is quite often necessary to fish very near to the edge of flat 'scaurs' or rock tables and this means that the place where you are fishing is constantly washed by a few inches of water as the waves break against the front of the rock platform and send a regular cascade of white, foamy water around your feet. In these conditions, a tackle bag placed anywhere on the rocks would either be washed away or constantly soaked. This is where the long, adjustable tripod

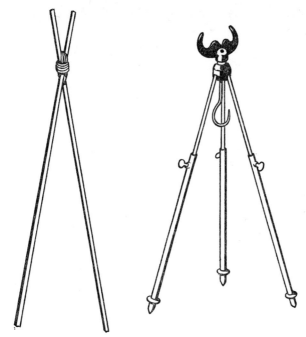

FIG. 6. Bipod and tripod with adjustable legs and baghook

legs prove their worth. They can be lengthened sufficiently to hold the tackle bag, which is dangling beneath the rod holding head-piece from a hook, well clear of any water which may suddenly wash around below.

Some very expert rock anglers who like to fish a fast rising tide and constantly move back every few minutes, must have a very light and easily erected rod support as well as a ruck-sack-type tackle bag so that they can move around without having to stop and gather up their gear every time they retreat. A very simple, but effective 'bipod' rod rest can be made from two five- or six-foot garden canes and a piece of stout cord. Simply cross the canes at the top about six inches from the ends and bind them into that position with the cord. The idea behind this rod support is that the rod, when rested against the two cane legs, forms the third leg of what quickly becomes a tripod. For lightning moves before a tide which is coming up fast, this two-cane method cannot be bettered. An added advantage is that they are very light and once the cord has been taken off them they can quite easily be slotted into the rod bag without any appreciable weight or bulk being added.

One wonderful advantage of a strong wooden tripod constructed from sound, close-grained timber, is that it is completely impervious to salt water if well painted and fitted (on the back leg) with a stout brass hinge and screws, and held together by a brass bolt, washer and wing-nut. The making of such a tripod, which will give years of faithful service on any kind of impenetrable, rough boulder-strewn shoreline, is simplicity itself and the cost is truly negligible. All that is required in the way of materials are three pieces of $1\frac{1}{2}$ in. x $\frac{1}{2}$ in. timber, 4–5 ft. long, a strong brass strap hinge with screws, and a $1\frac{3}{4}$ in. brass coach bolt with a washer and wing-nut. First saw off about 6 in. of what will become the back leg to give the tripod the necessary 'back-tilt'. Then, after clamping all three pieces together, bore a hole through them all centrally about 1 in. from the top of the short back leg to take the securing bolt. Saw the short back leg square across about 3 in. below the bolt hole, and fit the strap hinge to make the adjustable tilt-back leg. Bolt all three pieces together – the long front legs next to each other and then the short back leg last. An added refinement, if desired, to prevent the front legs from doing the splits and opening out, can be a couple of holes bored through the front legs near the bottom, and a piece of cord tied between them for greater stability.

Whilst on this most important subject of reliable, well designed monopods and rod rests which really will keep your tackle from coming to grief through being pulled over by the tidal flow, blown down in a gale, or dislodged by wave action round the bottom of your single-legged beach rod rest, let me issue a solemn warning against the very grave error of leaving your tackle unattended while it is cast out, in the hope that something will take hold. The trouble is, that may be exactly what happens, only the unknown thing at the other end could be much more powerful than you envisaged, and heave all the lot – rod, reel and rest – over with one mighty jerk and rapidly pull it into deep water and oblivion before you have the chance to grab it!

Perhaps you are having a quiet chuckle to yourself in disbelief? Surely such a happening is almost impossible? So to convince you and perhaps save you a great loss at some future date here are three 'disappearing' incidents all of which I can personally guarantee are true. Angler number one, a friend of mine, took a beginner beach fishing. Having set up his tackle, cast out, and placed his rod in a well designed monopod, he turned his back on it and began to assist the novice with his gear. A few minutes later, he glanced seawards to make sure his set-up was all right and to his amazement *it had all gone!* Certainly not stolen, because it was a lonely beach with no other human being in sight.

Angler number two, fishing alone on a quiet beach and retreating back towards the cliffs before a rising tide, discovered an old pram wheel set half buried in the sand quite near to him just back up the beach. Thinking he would remove it so that when the tide rose and covered it he wouldn't get snagged, he turned his back on his gear and began to heave the old iron out of the sand, and when it was loose he carted it up the beach and threw it well above the high water mark just near the bottom of the cliffs. A tremendous shock awaited him when he turned round to see if he had a bite – *there was just the empty beach where his rod had been!*

Shorecaster number three was a young lad whom I know, fishing in the company of his father and of course, like so many social minded anglers do, he was busily chatting in a little group about fifty or sixty yards away from his rod. Suddenly a shout went up that his rod was indicating a rattling bite. He certainly had just that. His rod was literally bouncing in the monopod and before he could sprint to it across the soft sand, it was jerked from the rest and went arrowing across the sand and into the surf to vanish rapidly from sight beneath the waves. Sad to relate none of these three sets of very valuable gear were ever recovered.

What happened? Your guess is as good as mine; but from

personal experience of almost losing my gear a couple of times, I will give three or four predictions of what could easily have taken place. A great bunch of floating weed or a sheet of polythene became tangled in the terminal set-up and took the tackle with it in the strong rush of the tide. Perhaps a small fish got itself hooked and began to struggle, whereupon a very large one grabbed it violently and heaved the gear into the sea. Or an inshore swimming shark fancied the bait, and of course quite easily made off with hook, line, sinker, rod, reel – the lot in fact. Please do not scoff at this last theory. Recently an angler fishing from a steep shingle beach for cod was almost pulled in by a 72 lb. blue shark which took his bait. Only after his friend had grabbed him round the waist and assisted him, were they able to haul in and land this unusual catch! Finally: consider this possibility, seals eat fish and fish are often attached to angler's tackle.

Lines and Terminal Tackle

After that lengthy digression, which although a little out of place, may give me the satisfaction of saving some reader a nasty shock – as well as perhaps quite a thick wad of hardearned pounds – let us now continue with the rightful content of this chapter and consider next the subject of lines and terminal tackle.

On the subject of lines for shorecasting – as with reels – I regretfully report that there are two schools of thought, but to make a pleasant change they are in no way evenly divided. The nylon monofilament disciples, like the ninety and nine sheep, are safely tucked away in their piscatorial fold all happy and contented with their lot. Whilst the renegades – the braided line users – all one per cent of them (perhaps to be truthful, a little more) cast away merrily on the shoreline confident in the firm belief that the line they are using is suitable in every way. No doubt the majority of aspiring shorecasters will tread the well worn pathway and load their first reel with nylon monofilament, but for those inquisitive souls who demand to know what the characteristics of each line are, I will very briefly run over them. The ever popular nylon (the monofilament part is just to ensure that the buyer knows it is single-strand and not multi-strand twisted or braided line) is cheap, has considerable stretch (which helps when you are a beginner making jerky casts) and, if it is of good quality, flows well off the reel spool and through the rod rings; which means it is smooth and of regular thickness and not 'watch spring' stiff. Braided Terylene and sometimes Dacron, which are the other types of line used for shorecasting, have very little stretch; occupy about ten per cent more spool space than that taken up by nylon monofil of the same yardage and breaking strain, and are rather more expensive than nylon. In order to write about fishing with a braided line, I have experimented with it. My findings are, that although its characteristic of having very little stretch is extremely helpful in feeling bites and striking the hook home, it suffers from a disturbing drawback which I will call 'reel-cling'. Briefly: it seems to bed down so well and snug on the reel spool that when a cast is made, instead of peeling off in a smooth fashion, it seems to jump in spasmodic jerks every few yards which is most disconcerting and, as far as I personally am concerned, unnerving.

At the beginning of this book (in Chapter Two to be exact) I gave a brief warning on the pitfalls of buying cheap job-lots of tackle at ridiculously low prices, and in particular I made mention of bulk spools of nylon. To the shorecasting tyro this quality aspect of line buying, i.e. poor, better and the very best, is apt to be a conundrum, especially when he sees a flashily labelled spool of very shiny new-looking line, at a bargain price, alongside a more sober-looking product at double or even treble the price for perhaps half or even a quarter the yardage! It is common knowledge among discerning anglers that there are only a few manufacturers of nylon monofilament. These firms sell in huge quantities to tackle wholesalers, who in turn, re-spool the line under a variety of brand names, which means that identical 'manufactured' line can be sold under several different names.

The crux of the situation does not lie in which line is sold under what name. The all important factor is, how good is the line? Quality control is the secret, and this is decided in the manufacturing processes – how well they are carried out – and not the label, the colour or size of the spool, or the seller's advertising 'blurbs'. A poor quality line may snap at the knots (which is almost always the weakest link) when just about half or even less of the stated breaking strain is reached; whereas one that has been manufactured under stringent quality control, may break only when the maker's breaking strain is nearly reached. You will find that cheap monofilament line invariably becomes deformed when wound on to the reel spool under strain, of a fish or snagging, but unlike good quality line, it does not recover and therefore jumps off the reel in kinky coils which is 'instant death' to smooth casting. Before we leave lines and their foibles, one useful tip when spooling a new line which seems horribly stiff and jumpy on the reel spool. Before you attempt to make your first unsure, 'heart-in-mouth' cast, tie a lead weight on the end of the new line after tackling up rod and reel. Then walk the whole length out on the damp grass of a sports field and reel it in carefully against the slight strain of the trailing lead. Make sure you lay the line on the spool evenly with your finger and thumb in 'cotton bobbin' style, and then repeat the whole business a couple of times more just for good measure to 'break' the line in, remove any kinks, and get it bedding down smoothly on the reel.

Leads and Weights

With rod, reel and line, plus either a monopod for soft ground or a tripod for the impenetrable stuff, we can now consider ourselves ready to cover what is known by anglers as terminal tackle, or the fish-catching end of the equipment. At the outset it must be realised that, of the multitude of leads or weights shown in the pages of the tackle catalogues, only a very few are suitable for distance casting. They must flight easily through the air without wobble, and be of the correct streamlined, weight forward, shape so that air resistance is cut down to the minimum. Air and wind resistance must constantly be borne in mind when end-pieces for shorecasting

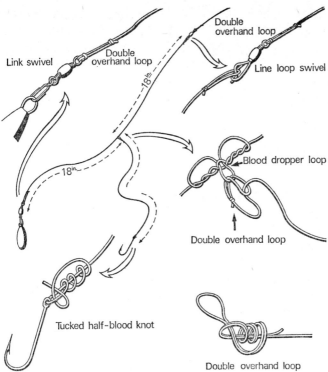

Fig. 7. Casting tackle set-up

are being considered. While it is quite possible to swing out into deep water just below a pier, harbour wall or rock platform, a great Christmas-tree-like appendage made up of half a dozen wire booms with separate hook 'snoods' attached, such a load of ironmongery, especially if fitted with a round 'nobby' weight known as a 'grip' lead, could hardly be cast thirty or forty yards before all the various dangling bits would slow it down and pull it off course into the sea.

Generally, shorecasters prefer just two types of lead; the torpedo, with or without wires; and the 'swivelled Bomb' which can be purchased plain or fitted with very long, pliable nose wires. To enable long, smooth, true flight casts to be made, distance casting terminal tackle is cut down to the bare minimum of bits and pieces. My favourite set-up consists of a quick release 'line loop' buckle swivel at the end of the main reel line, to which is attached a yard-long 'lead link' of slightly less breaking strain with a 'blood-dropper-loop' tied in the middle for the hook snood. The lead casting weight is attached by a further link swivel, and the hook snood, which again is of a slightly reduced breaking strain, is attached to the dropper loop by the interlocking loop method. The theory behind this 'reduced breaking strain' terminal tackle set-up is to cut tackle losses down to the bare minimum when fishing over snaggy ground, and it works like this. If your main reel line is, say, 26 lb. b.s. then your reel line swivel to casting weight link should be 22 lb. Dropping down to the hook snood, this should be of 18 lb. b.s. so that if the hook becomes snagged, that link breaks and you still get back your lead and the rest of the terminal tackle. When the lead gets jammed in a crack in the rocks or behind a big boulder and you are forced to pull for a break, then the link between reel line swivel and lead swivel breaks and you don't lose yards of your main reel line.

My 'casting-tackle' Figure 7 illustration shows just three very simple and reliable knots which have been tried, tested and found utterly dependable by a great many shorecasters of long experience: myself included. I am aware that all kinds of very fancy knots do exist in Seamen's Manuals and Boy Scout Guides; but these are intended to be tied in rope, cord or string. Synthetic fishing line, especially nylon monofilament, is quite a different proposition. Due to its mooth, shiny, regular surface and circular form, it is prone to a very distressing characteristic known as 'creep'. Unless all knots are tied very carefully in line which has been thoroughly wetted or at least dampened with saliva, and the coils snugged down neatly while steady tension is applied when tightening, a badly formed knot may result which will fail to remain secure under strain, or appreciably weaken the line at that point if it does hold.

All knots are weak links which is why they should be used very sparingly in shorecasting tackle. A well tied knot, in good quality line, should not reduce the breaking strain by much more than 10 to 20 per cent of its 100 per cent un-knotted strength; given in either pounds or kilos (usually both).

In a later chapter dealing exclusively with casting tech-niques, I mention the bloodknot (a double version of the half-blood knot which is illustrated in this chapter for tying on hooks). This is used in the main reel line for attaching an extra strong 'casting-piece' by some very expert fishermen to whom distance casting is of prime importance. I would not, however recommend any beginner to the shorecasting scene to attempt to perform smooth, effortless casts if his main reel line has knots in it – no matter how well tied. They always produce 'bumps' underneath the coils which are reeled on immediately above them. If the ends of such knots are cut off dead flush the knot is liable to pull apart suddenly and without warning. Conversely, if two rather generous 'safety-margin' ends are left on such knots these projections will produce unlimited overruns as they considerably hamper the free flow of line from the reel spool, at speed, when a cast is being made.

The golden rules for successful knot tying are: pre-soak the line or at least see that it has been immersed for a short time or well dampened in your mouth. Form the knot care-fully, leaving a rather long loose end. Snug down the coils neatly. Tension slowly and with a steady pull, while watching the 'spare' loose end for 'creep' – which indicates that the knot is slipping. Finally, trim off the loose end (not too short) only when you are quite sure that the knot has 'bedded-down' securely and will not slip and come untied. If in doubt, cut the line and begin again, until you are satisfied that your knot is perfect.

When you have hooked, played and almost landed a very good fish and lost it – as I have – because a 'doubtful' knot let you down, then – and only then – will your lesson in knot tying be complete!

Recently a wonderful innovation has appeared on the beachcasting scene: 'The Breakaway Lead'. By a very in-genious arrangement of four beads attached to the 'anchor' wires (which are not fixed, but swing about in their holes), and four recesses in the body of the lead into which the beads can be pushed to keep the wires in the anchor position, this amazing gadget has two phases of operation. With wires set to 'anchor' it works like the normal 'grapple' lead, but when a strike is made and the angler begins to reel in, the pull on the wires releases the beads from their recesses, the wires fold back and trail, obviating the 'plough' effect which is the great disadvantage of fixed wires. A cheaper, but workable version of this 'release' wire lead is the elastic band type, which dispenses with the beads and recesses and relies on elastic bands to secure the wires in the 'anchor' position.

One very thrifty way of cutting your terminal tackle bill down to the bare bones, is to obtain a sinker mould – or if you can afford the expense, several of them – and cast your own lead weights. Anglers who reside near and fish over very stony, rough, tackle-hungry ground will quickly save themselves from bankruptcy if they are fully equipped with a set of lead moulding gear. There is certainly nothing very highly skilled about sinker making. Anyone can soon learn to carry out this quite simple operation; but the sinker casters who perform in a safe and sensible fashion are very few indeed. Moisture and molten lead do not mix; and that is usually the cause of all the sinker casting accidents. For the maximum safety these few points should be rigorously observed. A great pot of molten lead should never be taken off or carried from its heating source. A small plumber's ladle should be used to dip out from the pot and pour the hot lead into the mould so that only small quantities are liable to be spilled if a mistake is made. The operator should wear goggles in case of 'spitting' and have his hands and arms covered with a thick jacket and gauntlet type gloves. Everyone seems to think that only the sinker mould is liable to 'spit' if it is damp, so it should always be bone dry and the hot sinkers should never be cooled down by dumping both mould and sinker into water. But . . . melting pots can also spit or even erupt like a volcano in a most terrifying fashion. The cause is usually moisture trapped in the scrap lead which you are melting, especially if it is a discarded water pipe which has been chopped into short lengths with an axe, leaving both ends sealed up and some highly dangerous drops of water trapped inside. This moisture when heated suddenly, very rapidly turns into steam, which blows open the ends of the pipe and causes an horrific upheaval of molten lead – in fact the whole of the contents of the melting pot can be splattered all around the room where the melting and casting is being done. Be warned ... open up all lead which could have cavities and hammer it out flat before melting.

Hooks

Last, but of great importance, we will investigate the hooks used by shorecasters, which are legion in design and number, and I have yet to meet a competent 'beach-fanatic' who does not swear by one particular brand, size and shape, denouncing all the rest as completely useless! The size most suitable for various species of fish is also a question around which a fierce controversy rages. Some anglers try to match the hook size roughly to that of the fish's mouth. Others dismiss this theory as bunkum and lean heavily towards the hook size matching the bait, whatever shape or size is being used, long shanked hooks for 'thread on baits' and short shanks for 'chunky' baits. When we consider that small flatfish manage to engulf the baits intended for cod and record size bass have been landed on dab hooks by anglers fishing for that species, I feel that no really hard and fast rules can be laid down about this item of shorecasting gear.

Unlike coarse fish hook sizes, which get smaller as their respective numbers increase, sea hooks begin at 1/0, which is just about $\frac{1}{2}$ in. across the 'gape' (the measurement from point across the bend to the shank) and step up in numbers to size 10/0 which is approximately 1 in. across the gape. Although they increase in number and size above that, 10/0 is about the largest a shore angler is ever likely to require. Greater than that and we find ourselves in the realms of the shark and big-game angler's tackle. Good hooks should be correctly tempered so that they do not bend or straighten out easily, but at the other extreme, they should not be so brittle that they snap when subjected to a hefty pull. Avoid hooks which are thick and very heavy in relation to their size, with very coarse, deeply cut barbs and badly formed eyes which are not properly closed, especially if they are a cheap job-lot box of five hundred or even a thousand. Buy them, and you will have faulty terminal tackle for life!

CHAPTER SIX

Personal Apparel and Creature Comforts

The cardinal rule, from a personal comfort angle, for all shorecasters who wish to enjoy their fishing, is to forget completely that there are supposed to be warm and cold periods called summer and winter. Dress up in, or carry (to enable you to put on) sufficient wind, cold- and wet-beating garments all the year round, because the date on your calendar does not really give any indication when you will need them most!

At times, I have literally sweltered in shirt sleeves in early November when fishing under high cliffs with a warm westerly offshore wind blowing and the midday sun shining so brightly I have needed polaroid sunglasses to cut down the fierce glare. Conversely, in mid-May, I have been frozen to the marrow by a cutting, off-the-sea east wind which drove before it showers of stinging hail which forced us to turn our backs to the wind and finally pack up fishing in utter confusion, because we could not bear to turn around and face the vile weather in order to keep an eye on our rods.

Some comfort loving shore fishers actually limit themselves to just a few venues with easy vehicle access. They then can watch their tackle from the comfort of an armchair in the back of a Dormobile, made cosy by a Calor gas heater, with endless cups of tea, hot soup and jolly jangling music on a transistor radio. For the ultimate in shorecasting one-upmanship, I have yet to see the equal of a fishing-mad family I know, who run a building business and in the winter cod season use a lorry to transport to the beach a portable hut on skids, which they move up and down the sand following the tide. Their all night sessions are made warm and extremely nourishing by the help of a glowing coke brazier (with plenty of fuel in sacks), a full camp kitchen outfit producing lashings of hot cooked food and throat-scalding drinks, and they have enough Tilley lamp illumination to put Blackpool promenade to shame!

Clothing
When approaching this knotty problem of keeping dry and warm on the shoreline, two separate aspects of it must be given rational consideration. On the one hand, an almost static angler who shuffles ten yards from his parked car to the pier edge to cast out his tackle (baited up with shop bought lugworm) just a few yards, can cocoon himself in layers of woollies, topped by an ankle-length oilskin coat, without the slightest discomfort.

In sharp contrast, the super-active, bait digging, cliff climbing, shore walking sea angler has a multitude of problems to grapple with in order to keep himself both comfortable, warm and dry inside and out. At the risk of offending all the makers of garments which they claim are both waterproof, and do not cause condensation, because they 'breathe'; I would advise them to put one on and try a three hour sandworm digging session, knee deep in mud, with the rain pouring down! From personal experience, I can truthfully admit that their products will certainly keep out the rain, but inside you will generate so much body heat and moisture that you will be a darned sight wetter inside than out! Now comes the crunch. Really, to be sensible, you ought to be able to go home, strip off, have a hot bath, a meal, a rest and a good night's sleep and then turn out in fresh, dry gear for your fishing session on the morrow. However, such a pleasant scheme is often quite impossible, as it means at least two days must be set aside for each fishing session – one for the bait digging and the other devoted to the carefree, pleasant part – the fishing. The only alternative is to do your digging wearing the minimum of heat-producing clothing and take the chance of getting a soaking, rather than attempt to be completely weatherproof while exerting yourself; because there simply is no answer to this vexing dilemma of the body generating excessive heat and moisture inside waterproof clothing.

If, for rock scrambling, cliff climbing, mud-sploshing and bait digging, you wear all the beautifully cosy, rainbeating gear in which you later intend to fish; by the time you have finished the strenuous part of the business you will be like a walking Turkish bath, with steam issuing forth from your buttonholes! And watch out for fibrositis, coughs, colds and a winter-long sniffle if you stand around in a freezing wind on a rainswept beach for an eight- or nine-hour fishing session in layers of chill-producing underwear and sweaters which are wet with perspiration.

As with fish catching tackle, there is the very pricey kind of angling outerwear which will, in addition to keeping you warm and dry, give you the jaunty look of a successful angler. Also there is a not so glamorous selection of garments, the kind worn by trawlermen, fish dock employees, agricultural workers and building site operatives, which are equally as good (often far more hardwearing) at a quarter the price of the 'angling-fashion-wear' garments.

Expensive, sporty coats with thick simulated sheepskin linings, fur trimmed 'parkas'; dazzling white 'Arran' sweaters and bright green lightweight waders may be the ideal get-up for a clean, tide-washed shingle beach, but such film-star apparel will take an awful battering if your angling and bait forays are done in an area of muddy estuaries, splodgy clay cliffs and rough, stony and often oil-spattered beaches.

The cheapest, most hardwearing and easily obtained shore-casting outerwear I have been able to find, and be comfortable in, is the black or dark green P.V.C. ship chandlers' coats and trousers with sewn and heat-welded, guaranteed waterproof seams. The coats are usually sold in two lengths known as full and three-quarter. With knee boots a full length coat will give ample cover, but the snag to such a long coat is that the bottom of it flaps around in the mud or sand when you bend and stoop while bait digging. There are two modes of dress to go with a three-quarter coat. You can still retain the knee boots but wear a pair of the P.V.C. trousers with the legs over the top of the boots to shed rain (and the surf if you are wading), or be even more waterproof down below and match your knee length jacket with a pair of thigh waders which will give you complete cover without the need for waterproof trousers.

A great advantage of this rough-stuff beach wear, is that it can be swilled down both inside and out, and then dried off in a warm atmosphere. This facility becomes necessary should the garments become thickly splattered with mud, fish slime, blood, sandworm juice and fish guts (a revolting, messy mixture, but one with which, I am afraid, every prospective all-weather shorecaster has to become acquainted if he wishes to savour the sport to its fullest extent).

Moving up in cost in the angler's wardrobe department we leave the bottom priced, budget class 'adapted work clothing' category, and enter the medium price range, specialist-wear field of shooting, sailing, hunting, climbing and fishing garments. Of these there is an astounding selection available in the sporting goods catalogues.

Some sailing suits, especially those designed for dinghy enthusiasts who suffer maximum 'wetting' are excellent for the shorecaster who is seeking all round coverage at a medium cost. Although the colours (Dayglo orange and a most startling yellow) render the wearer most conspicuous, especially if he is seeking to escape the hurly-burly of life and become part of the landscape, the top half (usually a one-piece, lace-up-neck, hooded smock) and the high waisted trousers, held up by broad braces, give great freedom of movement and good protection even in the foulest of weather.

In the super-tax price bracket, are one-piece hooded, custom-built, all-enveloping fishing suits which have an inner lining of thick Tricel wadding and foam, beneath an outer skin of the heaviest industrial quality nylon. These garments are absolutely waterproof outside and guaranteed inside to keep the wearer warm and free from draughts in temperatures down to sub-zero Arctic level. What more could you ask in shorecasting comfort? The one great drawback to all these 'super-heat' garments (apart from their truly formidable price tags) is that there are no half-measures with the wearing of them. If the temperature is really low and you wear one, it will do a wonderful job keeping you warm. However, there is no half-power stage – they are either on or off – so that once you have committed yourself to wearing one during a beach session, it stays on and perhaps you may range from very cosy during the early hours of the morning to tropically sweltered if a shift in the wind puts up the temperature appreciably. Having arrived at the sticky stage, the height of folly is to throw off your super garment with a great sigh of relief and fish with gay abandon for half an hour in your shirt sleeves, just to get your soaring temperature down a little! That is the foolish behaviour from which attacks of double pneumonia derive.

I really do believe that the happy medium in fishing clothing can be reached by having a roomy, lightweight wind and waterproof two-piece suit for outerwear and adjusting the thickness of undergarments – which give both warmth and afford thermal insulation – to match the climatic variations and antics of the angler wearing them. For instance, a great thick sweater put on just before a long cliff walk, carrying all your gear, and terminated by a temperature raising rock scramble to reach your angling station, will not only produce warmth, it will positively bring you out in a steaming lather. And that is certainly not the effect which you require. Far better to strap the sweater across your haversack and then, when you have done your stint of physical exertions, and plan on remaining almost static, put on the thick woolly and reap the full benefit of it in a dry, warmth giving state rather than a damp, sticky, chill producing one. Now for some serious discourse on what to wear underneath all these carefully chosen outer garments. Next to your skin, without a doubt, that great innovation made universally popular in World War II, the string vest – cool in summer and warm in winter – plus underpants of the same design, for all-round air conditioned effect. Here is a tip passed on to me by an old beach expert on the art of keeping warm. Go to bed the night before your winter fishing outing in the underclothes you will wear the next day and don't take them off when you get up – merely add to them! It certainly works wonders. For really luxurious warmth I think there is nothing to surpass the comfort given by a loose fitting pair of thick Winceyette pyjamas worn over a string vest and pant 'underlay' – well warmed by sleeping in them the night before. When your four o'clock alarm rings to summon you to fish a mid-morning tide, you will have not the slightest trouble getting out of bed because when you emerge to a chilly morn, your night-long store of warmth will appear to last the whole day through.

Hands and Feet

Before we leave the subject of angler's apparel and pass on to tackle transporting equipment, seating accommodation and that very important topic which I shall call 'beach-bashers' banqueting arrangements', let us for a few paragraphs consider the three most important parts of the body which must be kept warm, dry and comfortable. Otherwise, all else apart, they will reduce your morale to zero level, be extremely painful, and you will suffer some most unpleasant after effects as a result of neglecting them. I am referring, of course, to the extremities – your hands and feet – and last, but of vital significance, that producer of many ills if it is neglected, the nape of the neck area – wherein is housed your life line, the spinal column.

I do not know which is the more excruciating, wet, frozen hands or cramped, numb feet. If you suffer both simultaneously it really feels as though the cold hand of death is upon you and life is no longer worth living.

Discomfort in the hands begins through having them continually wet and then trying to force them into gloves to warm them. After a while the gloves become saturated inside and you are then actually putting your hands into what feels like soggy, miniature refrigerators! A long towel, worn scarf fashion around the neck, with one end hanging down longer than the other, will enable you to dry off your hands before putting your gloves on. For those anglers who do not feel at home in gloves and who prefer the bare-handed approach when they are casting, baiting up and handling their tackle, the 'sheepskin-pockets' idea may solve their problem. It is simple, cheap, and it works. Buy some sheepskin offcuts which can quite easily be obtained (they are often sold as shoe and car polishers), and after measuring up the pockets of your fishing coat (which for greater comfort should be deep and roomy), sew up two inner pockets of a slightly smaller size in the sheepskin and securely tack them, with large stitches, into the existing coat pockets, woolside inwards of course. This built-in glove-pocket method of keeping your hands warm is especially effective at night when you are fishing in total darkness with the aid of a small rod-end 'see-tip' light. It is on these occasions, when wearing gloves, that you rapidly throw them off to dive for your rod when a rattling bite is indicated, and they either end up wet, filthy and trodden into the mud, or gently floating in the tideline surf!

'Bait-digger's-hands' are a most painful trademark of a very arduous profession – and I am sure no shorecaster who does his own lugworm excavating will want to have chapped, cracked and blistered hands the same as the 'twelve hundred a day' men! If like me, you have soft 'clerky' hands (and I might add, a creaky, sedentary worker's back) a couple of hours on the worm beds with a sandy or muddy-handled fork will wreak havoc with the tender skin of your lily-white palms. There really is no need to suffer such punishment which will later affect your tackle handling efficiency. Before you put a hand on a fork to dig, invest in a pair of loose fitting, P.V.C. (they are usually bright red) industrial workers' gloves and then for added warmth, wear inside them a thin pair of woollen gloves. You may feel so comfortable while wearing them for digging that you will keep them on for fishing as well. They are certainly a most cheap and effective way of keeping your hands dry and warm if used in conjunction with a thin pair of woollen 'inners'. Even when they become rather 'high' and give off a strong fish dock aroma, they can easily be made sweet-smelling and decent again by a good wash in warm soap suds, after which they can be pegged out on the clothes line to dry in a warm breeze with the weekly wash.

Every shore angler I have spoken to has his own pet theories about suitable fishing footwear and how to keep your feet warm. One very off-beat character I know, buys his rubber knee boots three sizes too big and wears his carpet slippers inside them! Another devilishly resourceful type cuts inner soles out of those polystyrene ceiling tiles and tramps around all hot-footed on the beach in boots lined with them. According to the type of angling locations you fish, walk and dig over, so will your angling footwear need to be chosen to suit. If you are a much-travelling, gad-about shorefisher, you will need a selection of footwear ranging from genuine mountaineering boots, through the rubber boot lengths – ankle, knee and thigh – right up to those very 'with-it' breast-high waders which are standard equipment for keen bass fishermen who spend long hours out in the 'surf-tables' on suitably safe wading beaches, holding their feather-light rods and hoping for a monster bass to come their way.

A good rule to observe for self-preservation in relation to boots is, that the longer the boots are, the more water they will keep out, but the deeper will be the water you can get into difficulty in, and the farther up your legs or body they are, the longer it will take you to rid yourself of them if the need arises. It is foolhardy to imagine that you can wade in thigh boots through soft mud which comes above your knees. You may flounder around for a short while, but eventually you will become bogged down, for the very simple reason that the higher you have to lift one foot to progress step by step, the deeper the other foot sinks whilst you have your whole weight upon it.

Thigh boots, although they look dashingly piratical when turned down, are a floppily fatiguing menace to walk in, especially when the weather is warm. If you keep them at 'full-mast' the slightest amount of strenuous exercise produces a very 'hot-seat' effect around the posterior region which is most uncomfortable when you arrive at your fishing station and look forward to sitting down to relax. For many years there was no real cure for the 'sweating-cold-foot', so far as all rubber boots were concerned. Happily that situation, within the last year or so, has been magically cured by the advent of what are popularly known and sold as 'Bootsox' or 'Socketts'. These closely resemble soleless slippers, but the secret of their astounding success lies in their scientific make-up. They are made in two separate layers, an inner, composed of water-resistant acryl, and an outer, which is a knitted cotton material. The perspiration generated by the hot feet passes as a vapour through both layers, and then comes into contact with the boot, where it condenses to water and is immediately absorbed by the outer knitted cotton layer. The inner layer, which is resistant to water, does not let the moisture pass back and so come into contact with the warm feet and chill them. Each time these amazing foot comforters are taken from the boots the outside of them will be found to be quite wet, however, once they have been thoroughly dried before the fire, they are again ready for re-use, and they last for a very long time before they wear out. They should be worn over an ordinary pair of socks (preferably thin wool). Any competent chiropodist will tell you that man-made fibres next to the skin are most unkind to feet which must stand up to a lot of incarceration in rubber boots. You must also make sure that you buy your angling footwear one size too large, as the socketts are quite thick and will make your feet feel cramped if you try squashing them into boots which are a normal fit.

Headgear – and 'Creature Comforts'
Natty headgear such as countryfied deerstalkers, 'Moscow-statesmen' fur-lined 'bonce' protectors, jazzy striped wool bobble-caps, and camouflaged bush hats, are all worn with gay abandon by shorecasters when the weather is not too inclement. But when it becomes really cold and half a gale is blowing, hats, scarves and large turn-up collars do not effectively prevent draughts from blowing around your ears and stinging, frozen rain driving into that vital neck area

which is most susceptible to exposure. By all means keep your favourite hat on, but for added protection wear a jacket or coat which incorporates a really roomy, waterproof hood into it, with both a neck drawstring and one around the headpiece so that the whole lot can be tightly snugged down over your hat. This will ensure that only the bare minimum of your eyes, nose and mouth is exposed. This cover-all precaution is doubly important if you are a member of the modern long-hair brigade. A great shaggy mane which becomes soaking wet where it dangles down the neck from the back of a hat is guaranteed to produce untold ills almost overnight which could put a stop to future fishing for some time.

According to where you fish, what kind of transport you use to get yourself there, and how near it can be brought to your actual fishing position, will depend the amount of what I will call creature comforts you can take along with you. At some fishing venues which entail a very rough scramble both up and down rocks, or 'sploshy' cliffs, the very minimum of tackle, food, drink and comfort gear can be carried. It is quite a formidable task to do just the two journeys – one when you start and the other when you finish – without a lot of toing and froing wearily to transport a load of heavy gear which is not really vital to successful fishing.

When climbing or cliff scrambling is necessary, hand-carried bags are useless. Everything, except of course the long, rather cumbersome rod and either tripod or monopod, should be contained in a good pack or rucksack which can be strapped securely on your back. It will then not slip around and put you off balance and cause a fall. Under these conditions the ordinary sling haversack is not to be trusted. If it is heavily loaded it can suddenly swing on its single strap round to one side, or even right round to your front and put you in a shocking, unnerving tangle of arms, strap and bulging haversack. Do not under any circumstances consider the very foolhardy proposition of strapping your long rod and rest or monopod to your back load. You can walk over level ground in this encumbered fashion, but it is suicidal when you are climbing to have such a projection to your rear, where it can become wedged in cracks, or throw you off balance when you traverse rough ground.

Those great cantilever tackle boxes (sorry! I should refer to them as the advertisers do as tool boxes because that way they qualify for a lower rate of tax) look most impressive when you open them on a crowded beach and reveal a fortune in hooks, spare leads, swivels and perhaps a standby reel; but the availability of all they contain, in neat rows of shelves and compartments, is their undoing. While they may be quite a boon to coarse fishers who are far away from the sea (under umbrellas if it is raining), unfortunately every time you open one on a wet, windy shoreline, the contents get sprinkled with sand and exposed to the salt spray-laden air. The effect of such exposure soon shows in tarnish and rust not to mention a cranking and grinding of any item with moving parts. Far better to store all small tackle in individual tobacco tins with the contents shown by a sticking-plaster label. That way, only one item of tackle becomes exposed each time you require a new hook, a fresh swivel, or a different weight of lead.

Featherweight camping chairs with gay, striped nylon backs and seats, are wonderful lounging equipment for shore fishing, where they can be erected on a reasonably level surface. But their lightness is often embarrassing. If you are using one on an exposed sea wall, promenade, pier or on high rocks, anchor it down with a short length of cord and some bricks or a large rock, otherwise the moment you stand up to attend to your gear, a gust of wind will send it sailing away into the briny! Just recently a novel walking-stick type of four-legged outdoor seat which folds up into a long bundle has put in an appearance. Free from projections, with a weight of just $3\frac{1}{2}$ lb. this is the type of seating which the wandering shore-caster will find most convenient to carry.

After having observed the eating habits of shorecasters for many years, I have come to the conclusion that to some of them, the word fishing means one long, unending meal! Frankly, I am quite convinced that their eternal munching is somehow tied up in the age-old angling theory that immediately you pour out a cup of coffee or start to demolish a sandwich – you get a rod-rattling bite! It is a certain undisputable fact that lots of warming drinks and nourishing food do tend to drive away shorecasters blues, when the weather is horrid and the fish not co-operative.

There are two schools of thought on the hot food and drink subject. One is to take all the necessary gear and cook or brew up on location. The other is to obtain two or three wide-necked vacuum containers and short-cut the whole procedure by preparing the food and drink in comfort at home and thereby cut down on weight and the inconvenience of beach cookery. To hit the happy medium and maintain a sensible attitude to the whole business, some basic rules for what can be done and where, must be formulated and observed. When fishing and tide watching, so that a safe retreat can be made, a thermos flask and sandwiches are about all that can be managed. Any involvement with camping gas stoves and pans could be very dangerous as the food may claim your whole attention and the rising tide be completely forgotten. If fishing alone on a beach where the surf is running well up and back again, it is unwise to leave your rod unattended while you perform culinary miracles well back from the tide line. Of course the Dormobile enthusiasts who back up to the harbour wall have no difficulty whatsoever in producing three-course meals while the fish conveniently hang themselves on the hook! Every man to his own idea. The lone-wolf shore angler with his black coffee and frugal bread and cheese – and the piscatorial promenade chef in his mobile kitchen-cum-fishing-van with the full works – soup, meat, three veg and a pudding for 'afters' to fill up the cracks!

CHAPTER SEVEN

Safety Precautions and Night Fishing Equipment

The majority of really keen shorefishers spend a great deal of their rod and line hours operating in the dark, since they know that certain species of sea fish move very close inshore during the night, to browse around when there is the minimum amount of disturbance taking place.

Some popular summer holiday beaches, piers and harbour walls produce very little in the way of a worthwhile catch during the day, which often misleads the sea angling newcomer to dismiss them completely. What a fatal error! Quite often when the bathers have departed teawards, the deckchairs have all been collected up and sheeted down, and the small boats with roaring outboard motors are silent, a wonderful transformation takes place. The fish which have been patiently lying offshore, out of range of the civilisation-produced racket, begin to move beachwards, well within casting range. Some times they move in so close that the unobservant 'ton-up' 100-yards-plus casting fanatics put their baited terminal tackles well beyond them!

Take Care!
During the day, foolish actions by anglers who are either irresponsible or ignorant of the simple rules which all shore-fishers and beach wanderers should observe, are fortunately often under the observation of coastguards, harbour authorities, lighthouse keepers and quick thinking, public-spirited holidaymakers with powerful binoculars and an eye

capable of recognising a dangerous situation, so that help can be summoned. At night, in the dark, you are on your own so far as assistance from casual observers is concerned. Never forget that a spirit of self-reliance and self-preservation must be perpetually uppermost in your mind. If humanly possible, always fish in company, never alone, especially on rough shorelines where a broken leg or a bad, incapacitating fall could prove fatal on a rising tide.

In my previous chapters, I have dealt with the other aspects of shorecasting in a rather jocular vein, as I am firmly of the opinion that the weight of the catch is not the all-important part of the sport. Rather is it a very welcome addition to the great amount of sheer pleasure, enjoyment of good companionship, relaxation, fresh air and quietude which is the most important part of shorefishing. So far as personal safety is concerned, however, I wish to write and be read most seriously, as I feel a great responsibility for the lifelong well-being of everyone whom I fire with enthusiasm for sea fishing.

Before you ever set foot on any shoreline – day or night – investigate thoroughly each and every possibility so far as tide, wind, weather and a safe route to and from your fishing is concerned. Never on any occasion foolishly disregard good advice given by anyone who knows the shoreline better than you do. Read carefully and take heed of the written warnings on any notice boards which may have been posted for your especial benefit. The information given on them is certainly not meant to be taken lightly and nonchalantly overlooked on the first possible occasion when what they forbid is most inconvenient to your plans.

All this stern 'Thou shalt not' stuff seems rather out of place in a book which deals with such a carefree subject as fishing, and I must admit that in this age of 'doing your own thing' stringent regulations directed towards the personal freedom of anyone are rather candidly viewed as rather 'old hat'. However, with frightening regularity, certain dangerous coastal regions each summer claim a steady toll of victims who invariably imagine that all accidents happen to that ill-fated breed of humans 'the other people' whose names are mentioned on the television and in the newspapers. Here in York-shire beach walking around Flamborough Head at certain locations is widely recognised as being a most suicidal practice. Yet with frightening regularity, each holiday season (and occasionally in the middle of winter), people are trapped on the under-cliff by the rising tide. If they are fortunate, they are rescued, either from above by rock climbing experts, or from seawards by fishing cobles or life-boats.

Although our friends afloat, the boat fishing anglers, regularly receive solemn warnings in the angling press regarding the carrying of the correct navigation instruments, distress signals and lifesaving equipment, shore fishers and bait diggers seem to be forgotten whenever the wise, life-preserving precautions are being handed around. I have often tried to figure out the reason for this grave omission! Can it be that, because they walk about on two legs and do not venture afloat, they are thought to be completely immune from danger?

Extensive tracts of shoreline, whether they are mud-flats intersected by gullies, or gently sloping beaches with raised low-water sandbanks, are the most treacherous places to be lost on, especially when there is a great distance between high and low water marks and they are lonely and remote. Should a thick 'pea-souper' fog come down while you are out on such an unfriendly shore, either digging bait or actually fishing, then unless you are equipped with a reliable pocket compass and are forearmed with the knowledge of roughly what bearing you must take to strike out and find your way back to safe ground above tide-level, you could wander around for eternity. Looking on the bright side, on a safe gently shelving shoreline where the rising tide could not trap you, perhaps you may be a few hours late in returning home. Conversely, in an area of deep gullies and raised banks, with no sense of direction, you could, whilst floundering in the right direction, have misgivings and become convinced by a sudden deepening of the water (in a depression) that you were on the wrong track. You might conceivably turn and actually commence to walk back out to sea again!!! Just before we turn aside from this rather gloomy, but very important subject of shore safety, and approach once more the joyous part of the proceedings (fish catching) in which I will deal with shorecasting night aids, let us briefly consider a most unusual hazard which on occasions proves very dangerous to the rockfisher. In certain areas around the coast of the British Isles, especially down in Cornwall, when what is commonly known as a 'heavy ground swell' is running (usually the aftermath of storms in the Atlantic) it is highly dangerous to fish from rocky headlands because of the danger of being swept away by very occasional, but exceptionally large 'freak' waves.

The advice given in a number of angling books and articles on the subject of the dangers involved in fishing from rocks is usually very sketchy and non-committal concerning this rare, but very terrifying natural phenomenon. Quite often the writers say "When rock fishing watch out for ground swells.' Very good, and so you should, but the point almost everyone fails to take into consideration is that, when you have kept your weather eye open and seen one coming, if your immediate line of retreat is a stiff and very tricky climb up a steep rock face (with all your gear – unless you wish to lose the lot), what chance have you of making a quick dash for higher ground and perhaps safety, before the wall of water arrives and sweeps you to Kingdom Come? Be safe . . . and stay alive to carry on your shorecasting to a ripe old age. Stay away from rocky headlands and other highly exposed fishing stations during stormy weather or when dangerous seas are running.

Lights for Nightfishing
And now to disperse the gloom which I have purposely spread rather thickly over the first few pages of this chapter in order to produce the desired effect. Let us consider and assess the merits and disadvantages of the shorecasters' night fishing illumination. All around the coast on winter nights at shorefishing stations you will find that there is one type of paraffin pressure lamp in use which reigns supreme and outnumbers all the rest, by (I would estimate) at least ten to one. The far-famed 'Tilley Stormlight' has proved its worth

over the years as a most reliable, robust, economical and easy-to-operate source of illumination. If you are looking for a cheap lightweight lamp which can be dumped in the corner of the garage when summer comes, and then thrown on the scrapheap and replaced the next time it is required, get a bright tin hurricane lamp at approximately one-tenth of the price of a 'Tilley'. However, if you are prepared to pay a good price for, and look after, your equipment, and in return expect long, faithful trouble-free service, then a 'Tilley' will fill the bill. Unlike electric and 'Calor' or butane 'Camping-Gaz' lights, once you have raised the price for the rather high initial outlay for a paraffin pressure lamp, you are 'home and dry' so far as running costs are concerned, and apart from the odd replacement mantle or a new washer here and there, it will give you years of after-dark cheer and illumination.

It would be pointless for me to take up the whole of this chapter with a full description of the correct handling and operating of Tilley lamps. The instruction leaflet which you will receive when you buy one should be followed to the letter. A few times outside on the back lawn in the dark on a windy night as a 'shake-down cruise' will put you on the right track. The size and weight of the Tilley is its one disadvantage when a great deal of after-dark shore wandering, climbing or cliff scrambling is involved. As it is $13\frac{1}{2}$ in. high by 7 in. wide and weighs about 7 lb. when full (tank capacity $1\frac{1}{2}$ pints for 12 hours' continuous burning), you would be foolish if you were to consider it as the type of lamp which can be tucked away into your haversack without a great deal of weight being added.

To mount your Tilley efficiently and safely on hard or soft ground, various types of stands have been made by enterprising anglers. The advantages of having the lamp well up off the sand, mud or rocks, are threefold. It gives a much better pool of all-round illumination, and it is safe from the odd rogue wave which comes much farther up the beach than is anticipated. Also, and very important, it is well out of the way of large hob-nailed boots and rod butts which are apt to be swung around in a rather haphazard manner when the fishing becomes hectic. Nothing can throw a pair of highly efficient shore anglers into a blind panic more than the sudden dousing of their illumination as a wave engulfs it or a carelessly swung rod butt knocks it over to the tune of tinkling glass, plus a broken mantle which instantly plunges them into an unforeseen 'power cut' blackness, and sends them groping in the dark for their tackle bags in order to find their standby lighting.

I have seen many ingenious Tilley lamp mounting stands on various beaches and mudflats, some of which also incorporated twin rod holding rest-arms projecting at right angles from the main stem, a baiting-up tray just below the light, and even hooks welded on for the hanging of coats and tackle bags. Whatever kind of lampstand you make, ensure that the top carrying handle of the lamp can be secured and also that the base is resting on a platform, or is held in position. If the lamp is dangling loose from its top handle it will swing around in the wind, and if you are relying on it to shed illumination on your rod top your eye-balls will hop around in their sockets trying to keep a 'fix' on it. With a fixed lamp mounted fairly low down, the light from it can be reflected to shine up the length of your rod end by using an adjustable shaving or ladies' make-up mirror.

A good Tilley lampstand, if properly made in strong wrought iron, mild steel bar or heavy duty tubing, is rather cumbersome and heavy, so that its use will be rather limited to fishing stations which are quite easy to reach. The wooden tripods which I have described for use on rocks or concrete, as rod rests, can also be called into use as low-level illumination Tilley lampstands and they are very easily transported as their weight is negligible when compared with a metal stand. Around some coastlines, and especially on some harbour walls and piers the use of bright lights by anglers, where they can clearly be seen from the sea, is strictly forbidden as they are confusing, and a probable source of danger, to shipping. Considering that a well pumped Tilley lamp gives just about the brightness of a 200-watt electric bulb, this aspect of navigational safety arrangements is most important, and any

Above left: a good 'cod sea' on the Yorkshire coast. Winter afternoon on a rising tide, a short, 'bouncy' surf and an onshore wind. *Above right:* the joys of light summer shorecasting – float fishing for mackerel on Filey Brig. *Below:* traditional 'Scarborough' tackle in use on the famous kelp-bed and rock mark at Filey Brig

Above left: Morning tide on the Humber Estuary. This is the type of shoreline where a sturdy wooden tripod is necessary. *Above right:* an East Coast 'cod catcher's' coat – a cheap wipe-clean fishing garment of black PVC with heat-welded 100 per cent waterproof seams. *Below:* the ubiquitous 'flattie' is the fish most likely to be taken by shorecasting beginners who fish from harbour walls onto a flat, sandy bottom

Danger on the beach –
a reverse-taper rod
under full compression.
One reason why the
tackle should be
sound and the angler
using it aware of the
pitfalls of careless
casting

This type of sheer
rock face should only
be fished from in the
most settled summer
weather when the sea
is calm. At all other
times, *keep well clear* –
and stay alive!

The author with a thornback ray of good eating size (4–5 lb.). Note the thick piece of towelling to protect the angler's hand from the very sharp tail spines, and the 'tailored' rod handle and reel fitting. The cork handgrip is especially useful in cold weather, as it prevents the static 'rod hand' from becoming numb (as it does when gripping metal or cold plastic)

Above: pocket compass with luminous points and needle. The chain is non-magnetic and does not affect the needle. *Below:* a Side-Cast reel in (*left*) the normal 'reeling-in' position, and (*right*) in the 'casting' position after having been swung around on its special mounting

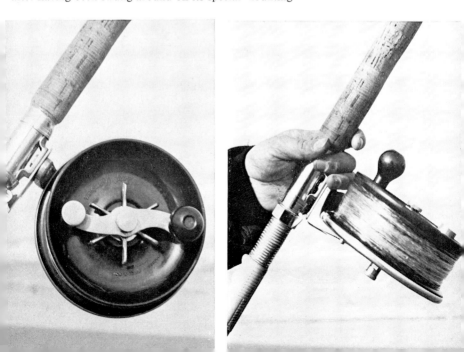

Above left: using the long-handled, three-tined sandworm fork in circumstances where it is best suited – on clean, firm sand. *Above right:* on mud-flats which do not drain the 'squeegee' method of surface water removal is often necessary so that the 'diggings' are not permanently flooded and the worms hard to locate. *Below left:* 'browsing' or ground-baiting from a West Country harbour wall. The tin contains an evil-smelling mixture of mashed pilchards and bran – hence the need for the tin lid nailed to a piece of wood to scatter it on the surface of the water. *Below right:* a lot of very good, 'free-gratis' bait can be obtained around harbour walls with a short-handled, home-made 'shrimp' net

Above: 'Black Gold' – thick, firm 9 in. mud lugworms. The shorecasting bait supreme, and invariably in short supply when fishing is at its best! *Below:* two popular types of shorecasting leads. *Left:* fixed-wire 6 oz. 'torpedo'. *Right:* 6 oz. 'bead' breakaway

Above left: a short-handled beachcaster being used with a fixed-spool reel, and a head-light worn in a way which will not encumber the fish-catching actions of the wearer. *Above right:* a 'rough-stuff' heavy metal monopod with the footbar sunk a few inches below sand will support the catch as well. *Below left:* gutting should be done in good light when the hands are not numb. Otherwise some very nasty slashing accidents can occur. *Below right:* the rod rest should be 'tailored' for the tackle. This is the ideal position for instant action

restrictions on the use of lamps by anglers should be rigidly adhered to by after-dark fishermen. Anyone who has approached the narrow entrance of a tricky harbour by night from the sea in a boat, will realise just how baffled a helmsman can become when lights of all shapes, sizes and brightness are bobbing, weaving and flashing in and out as anglers either carry and swing their lights, or crouch over them and then move away again.

Where such seaward-shining lighting regulations exist, boxed-in lights below harbour-wall level are often permitted, and for this purpose the fairly cheap and low-level illumination hurricane lamp will suffice. They are quite reliable, economical to run, and when they become thoroughly rusty and the fuel chamber springs a leak, you can pop them into the dustbin and buy a replacement without suffering the slightest financial embarrassment.

In recent years, some shorecasters have dispensed completely with permanent illumination while they are fishing, and rely for bite indication on a hand-held rod, or if it is rested or mounted in a monopod, they clip a 'see-tip' or 'glow-light' device to the rod end quite near the tip ring. There are various kinds, and they are quite expensive, but in view of the fact that they are guaranteed to emit a continuous light at a constant level for at least twenty years without recharge, they are a very sensible buy. They usually incorporate a small isotope tube or a phosphor/tritium gas bulb which is mounted on the rod end with either one or two small, plastic covered 'Terry' clips. On a pitch black night they really can be seen quite clearly at a distance of up to twenty yards as claimed by the makers. Just one small snag which I have discovered while using one. To prevent any accident when a cast is being made the 'see-tip' should be removed from the rod and then replaced. This is a wise precaution so that your valuable gadget does not fly off and is lost in the surf, or in some way causes a coil of line to become wrapped around it and a break-off suffered. The trouble, when fishing on a shoreline with steep breaking waves, comes when the rod-end light has to be replaced, as

D

this means that the rod end has to be lowered right down so that it can be clipped on. Usually during this operation the waves break on to the line, which has been lowered, and shift the terminal tackle from its original resting place, depositing it well down tide if a strong lateral flow is running.

I find it most surprising that head-lights have been used by miners, potholers and construction workers for many years, yet they have only recently been adopted by anglers as a worthwhile, free-handed source of illumination which gives a powerful beam of light directed automatically by the head to the area which the wearer is viewing. When buying a head-light for angling I am inclined to favour every time, the ultra-lightweight kind which fits on the head by means of a wide adjustable elastic headband. These invariably incorporate a power-pack battery container with a long length of wire so that the lamp can be strapped to the head of the wearer, and the battery container clipped to a belt worn round the waist.

After many experiments, I have come to the conclusion that the wire and the battery pack are best left outside the clothing, the latter secured to a broad leather belt by its rust-proof clip so that it is approximately in the small of the angler's back with the wire running up (and left rather slack) to the headlamp. If the headband is worn around the bare head 'Indian brave' style, the tight pressure necessary to achieve a secure grip can result in an unpleasant headache. This is best avoided simply by wearing some kind of hat to provide secure grip without pressure.

The reason for the 'outside wiring' effect up the angler's back with the power-pack slung behind, is to ensure that the frontal 'operating' area of the angler is free from encumbrance. Nothing could be more infuriating than to stand out in the surf reeling in a good fish, and as you bend down to beach it, the projecting reel handle catches your head-lamp wire, pulls the lamp off your head and the power-unit out of the unbuttoned pocket where it is supposedly resting safe and secure, so that the whole lot – your hat, head-lamp and power-pack are unceremoniously dumped into the sea! The height of indignity on such an infuriating occasion is to lose your headgear, your light source, and the fish as well, with perhaps both boots filled with sea water and soaking wet coat sleeves up to your elbows as you grope around trying to recover your lost possessions. Right now, I am inclined to offer up a silent prayer that to save further expense, you are wearing a fully waterproof watch ...

There are decided complications if you mount the head-lamp power pack underneath your coat and run the wire up to the lamp inside it. To switch on or off you have to do a sort of semi-striptease on the beach, and while performing such unzipping or unbuttoning antics you invariably give the wire a jerk which displaces the head-lamp and your hat, unless you have it jammed on tight or it is the kind with a peak and earflaps which tie under the chin. A timely tip here on the subject of battery conservation. Some head-light power-pack units incorporate an easily located (in the dark) raised switch which projects well above the casing and slides quite freely into either the 'on' or 'off' position. This precise feature, designed for easy operation in the dark, can also be your undoing when the lamp is stowed loose in your tackle bag with the batteries loaded. It is liable to get itself pushed accidentally into the 'on' position and burn out the power source so that unless you always remember to carry a set of spare batteries for such emergencies, you could be caught without a light. An easy way to prevent such annoyance, is to stick a piece of adhesive plaster over the switch while it is in the 'off' position and stow it away safely in the knowledge that it cannot be inadvertently pushed over. This plaster method also works when you are fishing and it is most important that your illumination does not suddenly become switched off by some movement of a haversack or bait container which may be slung over your back in close proximity to the head-lamp power-pack.

When ascending or descending tricky rock faces or squelchy cliff paths, and it is essential that the hands are as free as possible, a powerful headlight which throws a strong beam for a good distance will be found invaluable. What is more, if it is properly secured to the wearer, a stumble or a slip will not suddenly plunge you into darkness as often happens with a hand-held torch or lantern. There is one great redeeming safety factor which battery-powered lights have over all naked-flame wick, paraffin pressure, butane 'Jet Gaz' and Calor (propane) gas lamps. The electric lights are perfectly harmless if you fall upon them or drop them, especially from above on rocks, with your angling companions scrambling up immediately below. They may shatter and be quite beyond repair; but at least, unless they are great heavy-duty models, they will not represent a weighty, lethal, red-hot bundle of danger which can burst and scatter hot glass and fuel all around.

While on the subject of electric battery illumination for shorecasters, I would mention that the only really reliable torches for the very rough use which they will assuredly receive, are those very heavy-duty, drop-, water-, and accident-proof rubber ones. These do not rapidly corrode from salt water and sand treatment because they have no outside metal parts. All that can come into contact with the deadly salt water menace is either the rubber casing or the very thick, shatterproof front glass. Your 'never-fail' torch, however, will still suffer from annoying black-outs if you do not regularly check the batteries and also make sure fresh ones are carried with, of course, a spare bulb kept in a secure place free from damage (certainly not rattling loose in a tackle box among your casting weights!).

For sheer convenience – when a little expense is not objected to – I have recently been experimenting with a small butane (Jet-Gaz) lamp obtained as standby house lighting for the anticipated power cuts which fortunately did not materialise. This has the advantages of being extremely small 5 in. x 10 in. (with gas container fitted), and weighing in at the almost bantam-weight figure of 1 lb. for the lamp unit plus $1\frac{1}{4}$ lb. for the full gas container: a total of just $2\frac{1}{4}$ lb. Extremely easy to operate, this lamp has a built-in, self-lighting unit which works on the same principle as a butane gas cigarette lighter. The great advantage of this type of lamp is that it can be switched on and off as required, and furthermore the gas valve can be closed down to half pressure when a low level of illumination is required. Compared with the very economical running costs of a 'Tilley', the gas lamp is about ten times as expensive to run, and it only gives the equivalent of 80 watts, whereas the 'Tilley' produces about 200. Where weight and bulk are the prime consideration and ease of operation is also important, a small butane gas lamp will often fill the bill.

... And Home to Bed

A good long successful night fishing session under a starry firmament with a bright full moon riding high in the sky when the weather is fine, cold and clear, is a wonderful tonic for edgy nerves which have been worn to a frazzle by the eternal complications of present-day civilisation. Although I would always advise against fishing alone, especially at night on shorelines which are tricky to negotiate, there are times, on beaches which are gently shelving, free from gullies and easy to approach and depart from, when the very pinnacles of shorefishing pleasure can be reached by simply standing very much alone and relaxed – just fishing. Let time and the whole world, with its petty annoyances, go slipping past as you fish and quietly steal just a few very precious hours – opting out – stopping the treadmill for a short while, and getting off, or to give it an appropriately acceptable name ... shorecasting.

To return to mundane reality. Quite often, especially if you are able to fish a good winter cod beach regularly, you will in the most inclement weather, linger on all night and arrive home suffering from a mild case of over-exposure to the elements. There are various ways of restoring yourself. Some entail a hot mustard footbath and half a bottle of rum and hot lemon juice taken slowly before a roaring fire while lounging comfortably in an armchair. My special back-to-normal recipe will in no way offend the teetotallers as it is quite innocuous, but it is apt to prove rather expensive, as the initial outlay for one item of the equipment is fairly high. Take whatever you fancy in the hot drink, soup or alcohol line, and do arrange for your bed to be thoroughly warmed.

A good electric under-blanket or better still a variable-heat over-blanket, which can be kept on and regulated to a comfortable 'toasting' level all night (or should I say day if it is the early hours of the morning when you retire). As an added precaution against any indication to chills and stiffness – which is often the painful aftermath of standing and being buffeted by wind and weather for hours on end – take a good soak in a well-filled hot bath and then after a brisk towelling, dive sharply into your luxuriously pre-heated bed and sleep the clock round! I'll guarantee you will take no harm and awake refreshed and ready for another fishing session quite soon.

CHAPTER EIGHT

Tides, Winds and Weather

In an earlier chapter of this book, when discussing the subject of choosing suitable tackle, I recommended all prospective shorecasters to gather together all the tackle catalogues, trade hand-outs and advertising material they could possibly lay their hands on, study these thoroughly, and then spend quite a few hours of observant loitering in well stocked walk-round tackle shops. The best shops are the kind run by tolerant, practical anglers who realise that fishing tackle selection is often a rather slow, deliberative business, and in their wisdom, the staff do not rush up and press you to buy.

Alas, the study of shore fishing stations or venues and how that important trio of imponderables – tides, wind and weather – will affect them from day to day (sometimes even from hour to hour) cannot be forecast or catalogued in advance and published in easy 'armchair' book form. These phenomina must be learned the hard way, by spending long periods on the tideline; walking the beaches, scrambling over the rocks, and exploring the ground beneath piers or alongside harbour walls at low water.

The assimilation of what I choose to term 'shore lore', that vital know-how almost bordering on a sixth sense, which enables certain sea-fishing match anglers to sweep the board and carry off all the prizes with such amazing regularity, is very closely bound up with bait digging and gathering, tideline wandering, and keeping a very receptive ear always

cocked, listening in to that ever fruitful source of information
– the angling 'grape-vine'.

Tides

Since the tide is your complete master in deciding when,
where and how you can fish, or gather, dig and catch your
bait, a local tide table is essential if you are to become
thoroughly conversant with the 'ups' and 'downs' of the sea
in your particular area. Most coastal fishing tackle shops stock
handy, pocket-size tide tables, which are quite cheap and give
the required information appertaining to the local tides. There
are, however, some very superior editions which are distributed as advertising matter by shipping companies, ocean
towing firms and trawler owners in the form of diaries or
calendars. Try to obtain one as they are veritable mines of
information. They usually give not only the moon's phases
and height of water in feet or metres, for the port where they
are issued, but also carry lots of additional information and
conversion tables for all the major ports around the British
Isles. Usually the local newspaper at a seaside or seaport
town carries a daily tide-time but unfortunately it very rarely
gives the height of water figure, which makes the information
of only limited use.

Without becoming too technical, scientific or mathematically
confusing, let me try to put into something only just a little
larger than a nutshell (I hope) the lowdown on why at eight
o'clock in the morning you can be digging lugworms on a
stretch of beach, and six hours later, in ten feet of water, you
can be casting to, and catching fish over, the same ground
where you stood and did your digging! The one great bogey
in tide terminology is that unfortunate word 'Spring' which
means the highest or biggest tides – those which coincide with
the new and full moon (twice per month). This tidal 'Spring'
has nothing whatsoever to do with the season of spring and
once you have that fact firmly fixed in your mind, you are
well on the way to understanding what I will call 'The Bigs'
(the Springs) and 'The Littles' (the Neaps).

Gravity – the unseen force which pulls down and drops

your lead into the briny before it has travelled as far as you thought it ought to have gone – controls the tide. The moon has a very strong gravitational pull on the earth as it is nearest to earth. The sun, about four hundred times farther away from the earth than the moon, exerts much less of this effect. At times of new and full moon, when the sun, the moon, and the earth are all in a straight line, the combined gravitational pull of the sun and moon (exerted from the same direction or with the sun and moon on opposite sides of the earth) produces an exceptional force which causes a 'spring tide'. This happening takes place regularly, at fortnightly intervals.

At the first and third quarters of the moon's phases, when the sun and moon form right angles with the earth, the separate, uncombined forces of the sun and moon have gravitationally conflicting effect, so that they produce only a 'low power' Neap tide which does not retreat or rise up as far as the 'spring' tide. To fit in perfectly with the superb pattern of nature, the Neaps also fill in the fortnightly vacancy, which together with that of the spring tides, produce a full 'moon cycle' of about twenty-nine days – the time which the moon takes to orbit the earth in a west to east direction.

And now to come back to earth and resume our fishing, or should I say, our preparations for fishing, which is a very circumspect perusal of a tide table. First, let us become thoroughly conversant with the various signs and symbols which it contains and the information it imparts. Excluding the date and the various separate columns for the two twelve-hourly tide times a.m. (morning) and p.m. (afternoon), and the water depth given in feet or metres, the moon's phases will be shown against the dates. A large black dot (like an enlarged full stop) denotes a new moon. A circle symbolises the full moon, what looks like a double right-hand bracket the first quarter, and a left hand bracket sign the last quarter. A very broad generalisation which sums up adequately the tidal movements is: about a week of 'Bigs' or 'Spring' tides and the following week of 'Smalls' or 'Neaps'. The rise and fall 'Depth or Height of water' figures will provide much useful information as the water height gradually builds up daily in footage towards the full moon and new moon dates and then drops off again as it nears the first and third quarter dates.

With our entry into the European Economic Community on 1 January, 1973, a great deal of confusion is now liable to arise over the twenty-four-hour clock system, the battle between measurements in feet and metres, and all the tidal measurement boards and very ancient harbour wall stones with imperial measurements carved in roman numerals. From my observations of the locally printed tide tables, certain small, close-knit and highly individualistic fishing communities are determined to retain the a.m. and p.m. of the twelve hour clock. They will also continue to measure their fishing gear in feet, and the 'Height of High Water' in that traditional measurement as well. They flatly refuse to be bamboozled into accepting a change!

Before me as I write I have a very comprehensive tide table which covers the years 1972–3. Although the morning and afternoon tide times are given in hours and minutes and based on the twenty-four-hour clock system, when the switch from 1972 to 1973 is made, I find that the 'Height in Feet' column has been retained, but the figures, instead of being around the twenties (the predictions are for London Bridge), suddenly drop alarmingly down to fives, sixes and sevens. Did Old Father Thames suddenly expire on New Year's Eve and run dry? A glance at a footnote in small print assures me that all is well. Although the 'Height in Feet' column has been allowed to stand, the measurements have been switched to metres!

By observing that 'Height of Water' column in your tide table, you can get a clear indication of the difference between a 'big' spring tide and a 'small' Neap, in feet or metres. Where the increase is very great – say ten or even as much as twenty feet – then it must indicate to you that a 'big' tide with all the added height of water to move both up and down again on the shoreline, will have to be most powerful and fast moving, in order to complete its flood-slack water-ebb

cycle in the twelve-hour period, before the next complete
tidal movement commences a repeat performance. Fifty
minutes is a good approximate figure for a guide to the
delay between today's and tomorrow's tides, but of course
with your tide table always handy like a miniature angling
bible, the exact time and water heights can be studied continually.

For those anglers who like to dig their bait as the tide
goes down and then comes half way up again, so that they
can fish the top half of the flood, slack water and part of the
ebb, the neap tides are often too small. By that I mean they
don't retreat far enough to uncover the best and most productive bait beds. There is also a time factor involved which
works both for and against the angler who is prospecting
for bait. When digging bait on the ebb or a neap tide, if it
retreats far enough to uncover really productive ground, you
can rest assured that once it turns and starts to come back
again it will give you plenty of time to dig as you retreat
before the advancing waters, because they usually creep in
very slowly. Conversely, in some areas, the operation of bait
gathering or digging is useless on all neap tides because the
bait producing area is only uncovered when the really big
spring tides retreat well down the shoreline.

The advantage to the bait seeker of the fast moving ebb
for a big spring tide, is that it allows him to get on to the
digging or gathering area quickly and follow the fast retreating tide well down, sometimes to almost virgin ground which
is very rarely uncovered. But . . . watch your step immediately
after low slack water. Unless you constantly watch the rising
water level and dig facing the sea, you could be cut off and
have to try a 'boots off and flounder ashore' move. At best
you might have to make a run for it – abandoning all your
precious bait (and you usually have unbelievable amounts on
such occasions) and your fork, which would prove to be a
serious encumbrance!

So far as the actual fishing is concerned, Springs and Neaps
also have their characteristic advantages and drawbacks. Some
piers, rocky promontories, and harbour walls completely dry

out on the ebb when the tides are big, but conversely have a remarkable depth of water around them at the top of a spring tide. If the wind is favourable and the weather right, they can be fished with the waves almost lapping around your feet, but under adverse weather conditions anglers lingering too long after the strong flood tide has started to flow, could well be swept off or perhaps given a thorough drenching, and their rods and tackle bags swept away.

At the same type of location, when a small neap tide is running, it is often possible to fish right through the twelve-hour tide cycle without either retreating or advancing and always have a fair depth of water beneath you in which to cast your terminal tackle. Sometimes in calm, settled weather, rather dangerous rock stations, from which it would be fool-hardy to cast if the sea was rough or the tides big, can be fished in safety right through the flood, slack water, and ebb of a gentle neap tide without the slightest possibility of anything untoward happening.

Beach fishing presents a vastly different set of problems because the character of the shoreline can be almost completely changed overnight during a period of severe winter storms which coincide with a series of very big spring tides. Usually in settled summer weather, with calm seas, the beach is built up so that it has what is called in beach terminology, a broad 'berm' just on the high tide line, where the uprush of waves deposits sand and there is no powerful backwash to carry it away again. How the picture changes in winter when the storms begin. Massive waves hammer the deposited sand, high up on the beach, and draw it back seawards where it remains in suspension and is finally deposited well offshore by outflowing 'rip' tides and currents.

I will reiterate a former statement and give the golden rule for successful shorecasting. Study the tides and the shoreline continually if you wish to become thoroughly conversant with what is happening beneath the waves. Holes, gullies and troughs harbour all kinds of marine life upon which fish feed, and by locating them and casting his terminal tackle into them, the sea angler vastly improves his chances of continued success. Summer beaches are quite often very regular in their appearance when the tide is far out, and have no great variations in contour or water depth when the tide comes in. Once the first Autumn or early Winter 'rough-ups' have occurred, however, they may change beyond all recognition within the space of just one tide. Quite often a weather-beaten beach in winter will have two distinct possibilities so far as the fishing of it is concerned. When the tides are exceptionally big, round about the dead low water mark, there may be a steep offshore trough into which the angler may cast his bait and reap good rewards for just about a couple of hours, during slack low water and the first hour of the flood. At half tide up, he may be standing and casting on to a rather flattish section of beach over which the waves are breaking heavily (a sure sign of shallow water); but again, at the very top of the tide, he may have to retreat up a sudden sharp incline which will once more mean that he is again casting into the same type of deep water hole as he was at the very bottom of the tide. Shore-casters call this type of variation on a beach a high or low water hole. They study their positions and often mark their exact location with stakes in the sand, or stones on the cliff-top. At all states of the tide they can then ensure that they are fishing over the natural marine larders where the fish are most liable either to congregate or pass along. The art of shore-casting is not merely to find a safe looking, flat piece of snag-free beach and then after setting up your tackle and casting it out, settle back in comfort and hope for the best.

Some very observant and astute shore fishers make such a close study of their favourite piece of the beach and the tides, that they have a preconceived plan of campaign all mapped out, ready to be put into operation immediately the conditions of tide, wind and weather are right. One whole day is spent digging and bait gathering, and the tide (usually a big spring) is followed right down and up again – a full eight to twelve hours of hard work and observation – during which time every aspect of the shore is mentally noted and patiently assessed.

Casting distances to rocky outcrops, patches of mud, seaward flowing runnels, and clumps of seaweed, are measured either by pacing out the yards, or with a reel and some old discarded line and a stake. On the morrow, the angler, thoroughly 'genned up' after his day-long tour of inspection, can commence his operations at high tide mark and cast to points where he is absolutely sure the fish should be. Also, by making a couple of moves as the tide gets lower and lower, he can still be fishing over good productive ground, instead of arriving at the tideline without any idea of what the beach beneath the waves is like. He is not fishing 'blind' in the fond hope that he will, by a fortunate accident, have chosen just the right spot where the fish will be feeding. He also knows that there are no snags in the shape of great barnacle-encrusted boulders, masses of thick tackle-hungry kelp, or even perhaps some old rusty barbed-wire entanglements and concrete tank traps with iron girders set in them – tackle-tangling relics left over from World War II.

High Winds and Bad Weather

Tides are obviously the shorecaster's master so far as where, how and when he can fish, but the wind, that fickle, unpredictable force which can be either gentle and warm, or freezing and of tearing gale force, is certainly the all important factor in deciding *if* he can fish. Open beaches, exposed rocky shores and piers or harbour walls, which project far out into the sea, receive the full force of wind and waves and they are decidedly not healthy places for anglers or anyone venturing very near to the water's edge when a real howling gale is blowing.

From time to time during a very long career, ceaselessly studying everything written on the subject of angling around our shoreline, I have come upon an article about storm fishing which has caused me to have a quiet chuckle. The writers proudly proclaimed that they were never ever put off by huge breakers, flying spray and near hurricanes. They fished as usual and if their terminal tackle shifted with the powerful tidal flow, wave action and wind on the line, they 'walked' the lead along the beach – and surprisingly caught lots of fish!

One outrageous individual actually included a photograph of himself clad in a thin nylon anorak and wearing shiny 'city slicker' shoes.

To stand safely, well out of reach of the water, and watch a Force 8 onshore gale with mountainous waves battering at the beach or sea wall, shifting hundreds of tons of sand, shingle and stones, with the windblown surf flying all round, is a chastening experience. Angling in this kind of situation is quite impossible, and I am sure that before the conditions reach such a state of turmoil, the fish have long since departed to the safe sanctuary and peace of much deeper water well offshore. Apart from the fact that no lead of any size or pattern will hold out in such a tempest, it is often impossible to assess correctly where the reasonably deep water commences. The wind-blown, shallow surf runs so far up the beach and retreats such a great distance again, that a long, hundred-yard-plus cast will only put the bait into a foot or so of water, where it will instantly be trundled back up the beach to land at your feet, or be swept sideways into the shallows and covered over with sand, gravel or stones.

The shorecaster of long experience seems to develop a kind of magical sense, cultivated and sharpened over the years, which tells him exactly when the sea is too rough for shore-fishing. He does not have to waste time tackling up and experimenting with various weights and types of lead, before he is finally convinced that the wind, waves and surf are too powerful to allow the tackle to be operated successfully.

A great error which every prospective shore fisherman will make early on in his fishing forays, is to view the shoreline from a high vantage point, such as a rocky headland or high cliffs, and grossly underestimate the height and power of the waves, which when seen from above appear quite normal. It is always advisable before deciding on a fishing venue to get right down at beach or rock level, and then assess the suitability of the conditions from an actual fishing position.

One of the great and abiding drawbacks to all forms of sea fishing where only a limited amount of time is available (usually at weekends, public holidays and annual holidays) is the infuriating frustration brought about by the vagaries of the weather. It always seems to deteriorate and blow-up a storm commencing Friday night and lasting approximately until Monday morning. If you are fortunate and live on location – perhaps five minutes walk from the harbour wall or local beach then your fortunes are favourable, because you will be able to keep a very close watch on the tide, wind, and weather situation, and have a quick three or four hours fishing whenever your workaday commitments allow it. Travelling anglers are much less smiled upon by the piscatorial gods – they usually need large amounts of good cheer and faith and a rare brand of stoic calm to carry them through the harrowing and fruitless journeys they are often called upon to make in order to fish distant coastal venues. If it is at all possible, when you are faced with such a pot-luck situation, do try to establish some reliable source of telephone information, from which you can obtain an on-the-spot weather report before you set off with your expensive shop bought bait, packed lunches, thermos flasks, oilskin suits and fishing tackle.

On some parts of the coast a telephone weather report service is available, but alas, although the greater part of the information given is of immense value to the shorefisher, it is decidedly not specific enough to enable you to say your fishing trip is on or off. What is required most of all, and often you have to travel to the coast to obtain it, is a sound appraisal of the conditions and weather, fishing-wise, from a practical angler.

To conclude this chapter, let us now spend a little time considering how certain tide, wind, and weather conditions affect the shorecaster and his fishing performance, and of immeasurable importance, how the fish behave in relation to what is happening all around them.

Strong-flowing big tides demand heavy wired leads, the simplest of short snooded, tangle-proof terminal tackles, the finest possible line which is strong enough to operate the gear properly (to minimize tide pressure on the line under water) and if there is a good lively breaking surf, a long rod and a high position monopod are essential so that the line runs out seaward at a very steep angle and clears the drag and pluck of the breaking seas.

Small, gently flowing neap tides, if calm conditions prevail, can be fished with ultra-light tackle, the minimum of lead in the form of an unwired, swivel 'bomb'; and a long flowing hook 'trace' which is not prone to tangling because the lead will not be rolled around as it will make very little movement after it has been cast out and allowed to settle.

Generally, a rough, lively, well oxygenated surf with a strong tidal flow will produce sudden and often very violent 'snatch' type bites from the fish. They have no second chance to sample the bait as they are swimming strongly to fight the push of the current and are grabbing eagerly at all kinds of food items which are being swirled around them. Conversely, in just the opposite kind of situation (a quiet, gently rolling surf, coupled with a very slack neap tide) the feverish inclination to chase and grab is not there, so that the fish can take their time to investigate the various food items which merely float slowly along with the tide. In these calm conditions a great plucking and dithering of the line may be seen or felt, therefore it is essential to have a long trace which allows the taking fish plenty of leeway during its rather tentative investigations of your bait.

Strong winds play havoc with successful long casting. Especially so if they are side winds, which cut down your distance and produce a great sagging 'belly' in the line as the lead hits the water before you can reel in a little and straighten it out. Big baits with long flowing traces or hook snoods can only be cast very short distances in very strong side or head winds. This may not be such a great disadvantage as it seems because during such conditions if a very lively, well oxygenated surf is running, especially after a good 'rough up' the fish may be feeding quite close in – at a distance of as little as ten or twenty yards.

Gale force offshore winds usually flatten the sea and give marvellous opportunities for 'Olympic Gold Medal' casts, but often the 'dead water' conditions which prevail during such land wind blows, put the fish right off the feed, or alternatively, send them swimming way out of casting range into deep offshore water.

I have always found that the first 'half-way-stage' of a good onshore blow and stir-up to be most productive of fish. After the storm has subsided a little and the sea is only just manageable so far as tackle operating is concerned, two very dissimilar types of fishing can be had. One is the long hoped for, copybook stuff, when every cast brings a rod-tearing bite and a well hooked fish. The other, unfortunately, is what makes anglers sell up their tackle and take to golf or tiddleywinks! Although the fish are there and seemingly ready for your bait, the most maddening series of twitches, half-hearted tweaks and dithers drives you to near distraction. At last when you finally do manage to strike a fish, hook it and reel it in, everything is made clear. As you 'tap its noggin' on the rocks to dispatch it, a great coughed-up stream of half digested food comes forth, lugworms, shrimps, small fish and hardbacked crabs. No wonder the bites were only tentative, the fish are stuffed to the gills with churned up, after-the-storm food!

CHAPTER NINE

Bait: Digging, Gathering, Catching or Buying

If I am ever in my local tackle shop late on Saturday afternoon and witness the anxious 'waiting for the bait diggers' pantomime (a soul-stirring scene which is enacted with distressing regularity, especially during the winter months when the cod are running well and Sunday anglers are numerous). I am eternally thankful that most of my bait is self-provided, which entails some hard, back-breaking work, but a complete freedom from the vagaries of the shop-bought bait market.

Apart from monetary considerations, which are substantial in these days of ever-rising prices, obtaining bait free by your own ingenuity and physical effort is in itself just as much an enjoyable and enlightening part of shorecasting as the actual catching of the fish. The great drawback, however, to being the complete, self-sufficient 'angler-digger-bait-gatherer' is that age-old bogey of location. Quite often a highly rewarding fishing area does not produce bait, and conversely, some areas of extensive low-lying mudflats rich in all kinds of bait, have only a few flatfish and eels in the shallow water which covers them at high tide.

Choice of Bait
Some baits are favoured in certain geographical areas for the obvious reason that they are easily obtained there, but others appear to be popular only in clearly defined areas for traditional reasons, and the sea anglers who use them seem reluctant to experiment with anything else. Mussel and fish

strip are two hook offerings which immediately spring to my mind. Up here on the north-east coast, especially in the York-shire area, mussel is widely used by commercial longliners and rock and beach fishing shorecasters as well. Fish baits however, are considered a very secondary hook offering, to be used only when little else is available.

The one bait which dominates the whole sea angling scene, and incidentally keeps a whole industry and army of leather-palmed, supple-spined, thigh-booted diggers hard at work, is that much sought after 'blow hole and worm cast' shoreline burrower, the lugworm. The shorecasting fraternity absolutely dote on them and of late the demand has far exceeded the supply, so that in some areas along the East Anglian coast the bait beds are being ceaselessly hammered and disturbed to such an extent that the worms are rapidly decreasing and will soon be completely 'dug-out'. In certain remote areas around the coast of the British Isles, virgin lugworm beds exist which for ease of digging and size of worms are a veritable lugworm-seeker's paradise. Unfortunately, these very rich bait beds are far away from human habitation or transport facilities, and to exploit them commercially would be too costly. A grand scale lugworm-digging enterprise did appear briefly in Scotland some years ago, and the operators harvested the worms by using a tractor and a plough over worm beds which were so productive and extensive that it was estimated that even farm-machine type excavating would not harm them. I do not know what put this particular venture out of business. Perhaps it was the wholesale sandworm suppliers eternal bugbear – high transport costs and excessive delay, especially in warm weather, when the worms rapidly deteriorate and 'go-off' so

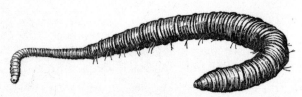

FIG. 8. Lugworm

that the infuriated private angler buyer receives for his postal
remittance a very high-smelling parcel which when opened
resembles not fresh, lively lugworms, but a revolting mess of
gooey blackcurrant jam!

Lugworms

So far as the angler lugworm-digger is concerned, the dice
are happily loaded in his favour. To make a paying proposition out of his labours, the semi- or full-time professional
'worm-winkler' must be a 'so many hundred a tide' operator.
Therefore he cannot afford to dig primarily for quality worms
but must always aim at sheer quantity in order to stay solvent.
Consequently, the professionals usually concentrate their
activities on the worm beds which give good average sized
worms, and definitely steer clear of those places where you
have to sweat and strain for perhaps two hours for just fifty
worms of truly enormous size!

Lugworm digging implements and styles vary from one
district to another, so the very best advice I can give on that
aspect is to seek out the stamping-grounds of the people who
earn their money at the game and closely observe them.
Ordinary sand beach digging is fairly simple and safe and can
be done with either a long-handled sandworm fork of traditional design – 4 ft. ash handle and three-pronged digging
'business' end which takes out a narrow, deep spit about
9 in. x 5 in. – or with what is known in the navvying trade as
a long, curve-bladed 'clay-shifter'. Both these tools work well
where a single-cast, individual worm digging technique can be
employed, as firm sand leaves clean excavations and the worm
tunnel, once located, by taking out a very shallow, experimental spit near the cast or 'funnel' can be followed until the
worm is seen, and then excavated from the sides to prevent
it being cut.

If the beach worm beds are very prolific and whole areas
can be found where the casts and blow-holes are very close
together, then a trenching method of digging with a flat-tined
potato fork can be brought into operation to good effect. But
it is pointless to shift great mounds of sand with an outsize

fork if only single worms are being dug, as the only excavations that need to be made, are quite narrow but deep ones, which allow the burrow line to be located and followed.

Mud lugworm digging is usually done in the areas of broad, low-lying estuaries or over vast expanses of treacherous mudflats, and can be a most rewarding but also an extremely hazardous undertaking, if the unwritten safety rules of the game are not strictly observed. The greater the danger, the less the beds are dug – and whilst that aspect of the situation is liable to attract some adventurous souls; to nonchalantly venture out on such an area with bait bucket and fork, but no prior knowledge of the type of ground and the run of the tide, is criminal lunacy which may possibly endanger the lives of many other people living locally, who will be called out to attempt a rescue operation, should you come unstuck and get into difficulties.

The digging of lugworms from a mixture of mud, sand, gravel and ground-up seashell is an operation which requires some very careful study, as quite often the bait digging area is very wet and squelchy, and it does not carry the characteristic indentations and wriggly casts which are a give-away for the worm, which lies in its U-shaped burrow immediately below. Often, when the wind is strong and in the opposite direction to the 'drain-off', an inch or so of water will accumulate and be blown about, so that the mud surface is flattened and all worm indications are erased. Likewise, during or after heavy rain, the above-mud worm casts will be flattened and the blowholes filled in, so that the digging ground surface is completely smooth. On such occasions, your shore lore, if you have acquired any, will be invaluable for telling you where the worms are usually to be found, so that you can 'dig blind' and obtain some bait.

Quite often, over exceedingly wet digging ground, where the holes made by your fork are rapidly filled with water even as you lift out the fork full of mud, so that you have no chance to see the worms, the squeegee digging method is the only one which is practicable. Briefly, a whole area, thick with casts, is worked over with a rubber bladed squeegee to remove the surface water which is then permanently excluded from the diggings by raising a small wall or ridge of piled-up mud to a height of 3–4 in. around the working area.

Some of the very largest and best-keeping lugworms are only to be found quite deep (2–3 ft. down) in a mixture of mud, sand and very finely ground, gritty white shell. Usually when such a productive seam is found, no further surface location digging or bait bed wandering is necessary. As long as the fork keeps grating on the magical shell mixture, the worms keep coming thick and fast until the bait container is well filled. With long experience, densely populated colonies of worms can be located, and if the correct line of worm populated beach is carefully followed, the whole of the bait required for a day-long fishing trip can be extracted from just one highly productive trench.

Keeping lugworms in a healthy, unshrunken condition has caused quite a few anglers untold grief over the years. Some advocate a thorough swilling in clean sea-water and then individually wrapping each worm in a tube of frequently changed newspaper. After many experiments (some of which proved instantly fatal to the worms) I have found that in cold weather freshly dug mud-lugworms will keep for four or five days or even a week, if laid out on seawater wetted sacking arranged in wooden trays on a cold concrete garage floor, well away from the light. The worms should be frequently inspected for fatalities(which are removed) and the live ones turned over regularly to keep them from drying out and shrinking.

In hot summer weather lugworms are a very chancy bait to attempt to keep in good condition for even just a day or so. They will stay in fairly good shape if well wrapped in paper and stored in the salad crisper compartment of an ordinary household refrigerator (wife, mother or landlady permitting). If you go the whole hog and deep-freeze them rock hard – watch out for squalls when you thaw them out preparatory to your fishing trip. Once again, like the disgusted angler who orders bait which arrives long overdue, they could qualify for a first prize in a jam contest!

Ragworms

Not quite as widely used (perhaps because it is not so readily available in all locations to professional diggers as lugworm), the ragworm runs a good popular second in the sea bait 'worm stakes'. You will I am sure, once you begin your lugworm digging, run across and fork out the odd white ragworm – something which immediately reminds you of a flat centipede. Retain them in a separate wooden box, in their small sizes they are wonderful flatfish and mullet bait, if mounted on a small, fine-wired hook.

In its giant sizes, the King Ragworm – fearsome beasts with blood-drawing pincers in their head-piece – can be obtained in sizes around a foot long, some even a full half-yard! Whilst the lesser red ragworm brethren are commonly found in mixtures of firm mud, sand and shingle on the tideline zone of estuaries, creeks and harbours, the real 'snaky' dark green King-Rag usually inhabit the bottom littoral zone areas which are only uncovered by the very low ebbs of Spring tides. They are an extremely tough hook offering which in their larger sizes can be cut up into several baits. These are not readily cast off, or nibbled from the hook by the lesser varieties of fish which may sample them before the real rod-benders finally gulp them down.

Do not mix your lugworm and ragworm baits. Store them both in lidded wooden containers to keep out the sunlight and the rain when your bait container is in use out of doors. Fresh water is sudden death to both these species of marine worms.

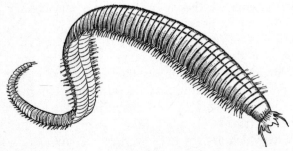

FIG. 9. Ragworm

Ragworms are best kept alive in a cool place in a mixture of wet mud and damp seaweed. They should be given daily attention in the form of removing the 'corpses' and changing their 'bedding' and ensuring that this does not dry out. From time to time in various angling publications I have read short articles on the subject of obtaining bait, in which the writers are illustrated with sleeves rolled well up, diving both hands into thick harbour mud to obtain ragworms; or kneeling on rocks groping around beneath the seaweed for crabs. Such practices may have been quite safe forty or fifty years ago before the curse of non-returnable bottles arrived to menace our shoreline scene. Nowadays, a bare-handed or bare-footed approach to anything along the seashore is decidedly foolish. On open beaches it is possible to keep a weather-eye constantly open for those very lethal half-broken bottles which have formidable upstanding spikes of glass. Around harbours, among soft, concealing mud and thick weed, the naked handed and footed approach to bait gathering is definitely a chancy business.

Mussels

Up here on the Yorkshire coast we are great mussel users. We even have a rule of thumb bait guide which states: 'Mussel over rock and weed, worm on mud and sand.' I honestly do believe that the majority of shorecasting anglers are apt to avoid shellfish baits for the simple reason that they detest the rather skilful knifework which has to be carried out in order to extract the innards cleanly in an undamaged state so that they can be mounted on a hook. A further snag which they also envisage with soft shellfish baits is their 'staying on the hook' power, which I readily admit is rather low if they are carelessly draped over the hook bend and allowed to dangle during the casting operation. What is required is a little ingenuity plus some 'rotten cotton' or red wool-and-nylon for binding, which should not truss up the bait in a cotton vest or red woolly pullover, but just have enough turns to keep the bait firmly in place during casting.

Mussels are a wonderful stand-by bait, and unlike the

various marine worms, they can usually be picked up at low tide on many beaches, from rocks, piling, sewer pipes and pier supports, without a great deal of physical effort. I have been able to keep mussels alive in their shells for weeks on end, in frequently changed salt water, by feeding them on a handful of fine oatmeal or even rolled oats put in the water once a week. For the less energetic souls who also have a taste for boiled mussels, the fishmonger-bought variety which are safe for eating are a boon. Some anglers take great pains to extract them all from their shells before they set off to fish, and store ready for the hook in mussel juice in a screwtopped jar. I am rather stingy, and 'skein' each mussel as and when required. Then when I arrive home with quite a number of mussel leftovers still alive in their shells, it is a simple matter to pop them in a pan and after cooking for about twenty minutes, perform on them with a fork, after dousing them well with vinegar, salt and pepper!

A great many slashed fingers and sliced palms have been suffered by anglers who are possessed of razor-sharp knives but not the faintest idea of how mussels should be opened. After serving my time as a lad to a longline fisherman on the coast, and having to deal with a whole sack of mussels at great speed, I can thoroughly recommend the following method of extracting them. The knife, and especially the blade, is all-important. The handle should fit the hand comfortably and the blade should be short, thin, bendy and very sharp with a good point. Whatever else you do, please refrain from holding the mussel tight in your palm with the flat edge up and digging at it with the knife in an attempt to gouge or prize it open. Such antics will bring about a very speedy visit to the local casualty station for several stitches and a long lay-off from fishing!

Take the mussel between thumb and forefinger in the opposite hand to that with which you wield the knife. With the mussel point away from you, the flat side on the ball of your thumb, and the curved hinge side towards your forfinger. To insert the knife safely, push with the thumb and press against the shell with the index finger, so that the top

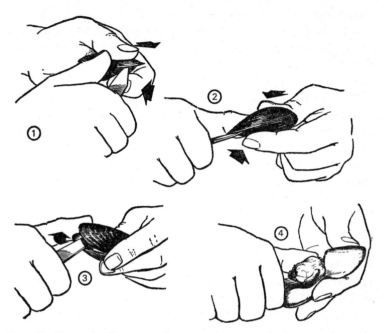

Fɪɢ. 10. Four simple steps when opening mussels (arrows show the direction of pressure with fingers and knife).

half slides sideways and a small amount of it overlaps the bottom shell. Now insert the knife point upwards on the curve just behind the hinge and slide all round the shell so that the holding flesh and part of the mussel foot is severed. The top shell can now be lifted and laid back while the knife point goes to work on the bottom half, and with a circular, all-round scraping, cutting motion completely removes the whole mussel from the shell. With practice a really flowing style of mussel extracting can be acquired in a few hours; but one point should be clearly borne in mind. It is fatal to attempt to operate with a sharp knife either on bait or in the process of gutting fish when your hands are numb with cold. You can almost sever your fingers in such circumstances, because if the light is bad, you can slice away at your numb flesh without feeling any pain until a great blood-gushing gash has been made.

Razor Fish

While on the subject of sharp knives and cuts, let us turn our thoughts appropriately to a very fine bait: the 'Razor Fish' — freely obtained in some areas from the same location as the 'King Ragworm'; i.e. the lowest of the spring tidelines, at the bottom of the littoral zone. That truly arctic winter of 1962/3 polished off lots of lobsters, conger eels, lug- and ragworms and alas, razor fish as well, which could be seen literally thick underfoot and dead on the tidelines in some hard hit, very exposed areas. If you see a jet of water squirting up at intervals from a keyhole shaped depression in the sand at very low water marks, you have found our friend the razor fish. There are two methods of extracting them in an undamaged condition – the salt, and the spear or wire. Don't try a great slashing dig with your spade or lugworm fork. The razor fish will be just too quick for you and squirt himself by jet propulsion very quickly down his burrow. If you are fortunate and do make contact you will chop it and shatter the shell, whereas the idea is to remove the razor fish whole and alive.

The salt treatment sounds like a music hall joke – highly amusing and impracticable; but I assure you as an accomplished 'salt dropper' that it really works. All that is required is a drum of ordinary table salt, a receptacle for the catch and real faith in what would appear to be a nonsensical method of operating. After locating the squirting 'razor', approach its hole carefully; pour down it a good 'pinch' of

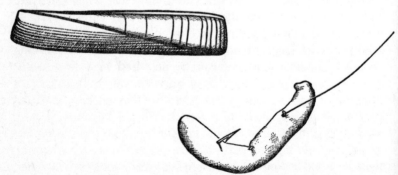

Fig. 11. Razor fish shell, and contents on hook

salt and await developments. Whether it is irritated beyond endurance or persuaded that the tide is coming up, I really don't know; but it will certainly pop about halfway out quite suddenly and allow you craftily to push in your spade blocking the burrow just beneath it, and then, as the razor is safely trapped at surface level, it can be withdrawn at leisure.

'Wiring' or 'spearing' is a fine art, to be taken seriously and done with great concentration. The idea is to find a hole squirting and after determining, by careful examination, at what angle it runs (they are not all vertical), slide down it a 2–3 ft. length of stiff wire with a hook bent into the end (cycle-spoke thickness, mild steel wire is fine) or an appropriate piece of thin steel rod, the end of which has been flattened slightly and filed to form a small barb. You can feel the extracting instrument entering the soft flesh as you insert it into the burrow. When you judge that the spear has passed right down the length of the razor fish, give it a full 90° turn and smoothly withdraw. If correctly operated, you should have the complete shell fish impaled and secured by the barb (or hook) in the wire being caught in the lower hinge of the shell. Always operate these two tools without any form of handle other than a wrapping of rag to save your palm from being pierced. The idea behind this little tip is to ensure the razor fish can be slid up the extracting tool and removed cleanly with the minimum amount of damage. Otherwise you might have to twist and heave it off the barb thereby ruining its condition for attachment to the hook.

Other Baits
Quite a good selection of other shell fish, apart from mussels and razors, can be gleaned from the shoreline by picking and digging. In the case of the rock, mud and chalk boring piddock, you can resort to 'jemmying' (with a short crowbar) or hammering and chiselling them out! Every aspiring shore-caster should be prepared to experiment with a variety of shellfish baits, as they can all be called upon at times, when the ever popular lugworms are very scarce in the bait shops, or inconveniently timed tides make safe digging in daylight

an impossibility. The one great advantage of shellfish baits which have been removed from their natural housing, is that they can be made up in separate plastic bags and stored for long periods in the family fridge under the guise of food items without the fastidious womenfolk of the household becoming alarmed and hygiene minded over them, as they do when the odious subject of 'lugworms in the icebox' is broached.

The far-famed, match winning sea bait, the 'soft' or 'peeler' crab, is one which is monumentally difficult to obtain regular supplies of (despite unlimited cash or untiring personal efforts). It is also difficult to preserve them successfully in goodly numbers from the summer, when they are freely available, until the winter when they are worth their weight in gold! As a fish catcher, in some areas the 'peeler' crab reigns supreme as the most attractive of baits. Nevertheless, it is not an easy bait to fish with, as it must be carefully mounted on the hook (elasticated thread is a very good 'crab-binder'), and cast out with a smooth, easy style which does not dislodge it.

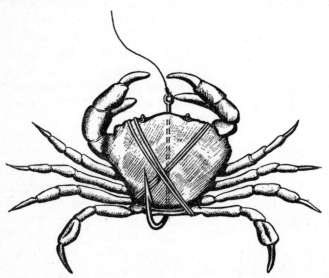

FIG. 12. Mounting a peeler crab on a hook, with a securing band of elasticated thread

High summer is 'peeler' crabbing time, when they swap their suits of armour for a larger one, gradually taking shape underneath the old one, which is then abandoned. Spring tides are the ones to work at low water, when the most secret of crab hiding places are uncovered and accessible. You can easily recognise the rather timid and very vulnerable 'softies'; they do not show fight with raised, open claws, but hide themselves away until their shells have time to harden, when they are ready to enter into battle again. All those curtains of seaweed hanging over the edges of rocks around shallow, low water pools, should be lifted and peered under. The prospective crabber should equip himself with a lidded wooden box, or at least a deep, well perforated polythene bucket which can then be stood in the water to refresh the crabs already caught.

Once more a word of warning, which could save you a finger end or two or even your life; if the tide is rising fast and you are working right down near the water's edge. Despite what you may read on the subject of bait gathering, never emulate some of the 'expert' authors and plunge your hands into nooks, crannies or deep recesses and feel around for crabs. A really big 'edible' can crush and trap your hand against the top of the burrow by flexing its legs and front claws, and even a 'baby' conger eel of a few pounds, if you thrust your fingers into its jaws, could clamp them tight and hold you immobile until the rising tide eventually put you out of your misery. An old blunt gaff or even a very makeshift crabhook made from thick, bendable fencing wire, will serve as a good crab extracting tool. It can be used up 'blind alleys' and anywhere where a 'finger nosher' could be hiding all innocent and placid until your groping hand poked it in the eye, and caused it to retaliate in a very painful and disastrous manner!

One very revolutionary baiting method which I am sure has come to sea fishing via the coarse anglers who have taken to saltwater, is the light tackle, free-lined (just line, hook and bait) livebait style of angling. This method is particularly adaptable to live sand eels, any small fish which can be either

FIG. 13. A baited drop-net

hand caught or netted from rock pools, and of course those two long established sea livebaits, prawns and shrimps, which can be taken with a baited 'drop-net' or individually captured by the use of a hand net. For fishing over dense kelp beds, weed tangles and rough rocky bottoms, a small live fish bait suspended beneath a torpedo-shaped float, offering the minimum resistance to a taking fish, is quite often the only answer to the infuriating problem of constant snagging.

A long time ago, before commercial fishermen became aware of its value, and we in this island home thought that the only sea-food worth eating was fried fish with lashings of chips (or when on holiday at the seaside, small plates of highly salted, peppered and vinegar-soaked mussels, cockles and whelks), a great deal of squid, octopus and cuttlefish was trawled up from the depths and went to waste or was thrown back into the sea because there was no demand for it. Today things have changed. Not only do we have quite an army of mollusc fanciers from overseas now staying permanently with us, but suddenly sea anglers have discovered the bait potential for this rather tough, rubbery, 'stay-on-the-hook' stuff, and are clamouring for it.

FIG. 14. Torpedo-shaped float

Squid tentacles (which waver in a tempting fashion) and the body, when cut up into strips, certainly make a very durable shorecasting bait which will not cut down your casting distance or part company with the hook if a rather jerky cast is made. It is wonderful as a 'convenience' bait; a polythene wrapped packet can be bought from the tackle shop and stored away in the fridge without smell or obnoxious appearance, until such time as it is required for use.

Those three popularly recognised 'oily' bait fish, herring, mackerel and pilchard, have a very mixed reception among shore fishers up and down the country. Along the south coast and around Cornwall where they are netted, or in the case of mackerel taken in goodly numbers by 'feathering' with a multi-hook rig, they are very highly esteemed as a bait fish, and indeed they do seem to take fish in much greater quantity than elsewhere. One explanation is the theory of fish becoming 'educated' to a certain bait if enough of it finds its way into their habitat from fish quays, herring and pilchard

E

factories, and the waste pipes of processing plants. I seriously suggest that all shorefishers make a very thorough survey of their local waters with this thought in mind, as the findings from such investigations may be a very clear pointer to what bait will be most acceptable to your quarry. Do not be dismayed if you come up with some very 'offbeat' answers to your enquiries. I know of one particular district where the vegetable effluent from a canning factory is pumped into a small secluded creek and the scavenging sea fish in that area readily accept tinned green peas as a hook offering!

CHAPTER TEN

Casting Techniques

Before I make even one slight suggestion on the subject of casting, I would like to pass on just a few words of warning regarding the vitally important aspect of safety, so far as 'break-offs' and flying leads are concerned. If you have ever witnessed the hair-raising flight of a 6 oz. chunk of death-dealing lead with trailing hooks attached, whistling along at head-level down a crowded jetty, finally to bury itself in the upright wooden planking of a harbour-master's hut, you would be quite prepared to give very serious consideration to the prevention of such happenings for the rest of your life!

Shorecasters seldom get hit by their own leads; as they are in the centre of the action. It is usually some unsuspecting angler up the beach in the 'fall-out' area who gets clobbered. Or on lonely beaches, an innocent soul walking his dog along the shoreline perhaps a quarter of a mile away! Remember that a lead which travels about a hundred yards in approximately three seconds, is moving at over sixty miles per hour. The impact, if it should hit anyone immediately after being released (by either a 'break-off' in the cast 'build-up', or the forward 'power-drive' as it begins its outward journey), would amount to several tons per square inch for a 6 oz. torpedo shaped projectile. As a parting shot (if you will pardon such a gruesome pun) there is on record the case of an angler who was hit in the head by a flying 6 oz. torpedo-shaped 'wired' lead. It partially penetrated his skull and was only prevented from completely entering his head by the projecting, off-set wires which doubtless saved his life, as the lead had literally to be dug from its deeply embedded position.

As an added precaution, I feel it my duty to explain that there are also several types of 'Tournament' cast, where distance, and not safety, is the prime consideration. These casts are decidedly not suitable for shorefishing where other anglers are in close proximity. If you read such remarks as 'Before the cast is explained, it must be understood that it is dangerous', or 'If the line breaks the lead is liable to fly off anywhere in a 270° arc', and even: 'I see no reason why this cast cannot be used for fishing as long as it is performed on a smooth, uncrowded beach'; then it should be crystal clear that such very dangerous antics cannot sensibly be considered as permissible behaviour on a public shoreline!

Lest anyone at this point should hastily put my book down and rush off for a suit of armour, a crash hat and a fully comprehensive personal insurance policy, let us now turn to the subject of 'common-sense' casting and the best way to set about becoming efficient at it. Although I have implored all prospective shorecasters to make a very close study of tackle catalogues, so far as beginners and casting are concerned I would strongly advise against paying too much attention to what are known as 'rod performance reports' and 'tournament casting distance tables'. Intense preoccupation with 'measured yardage' in your initial stages will lead to a distressing complaint suffered by legions of disillusioned sea fishermen, which I will call 'long distance lunacy'. Some casting court devotees have very little, if indeed any, interest in fishing and treat distance casting as a glorified form of athletics, rather than an exploratory branch of fishing tackle performance. From time to time, with monotonous and distressing regularity, 'gimmick' rods of the most unorthodox fishing design appear on the tackle market in a burst of unprecedent publicity. The makers claim instant 'over the ton' casting ability for any angler – provided he can raise the somewhat fearsome figure on the price tag! Be not misled; a smooth 'bowling green' casting court on a warm, sunny, windless day, bears not the slightest resemblance to a rocky shoreline, with a gale force cross-wind blowing on a pitch black night.

Before me as I write, I have a set of sequence photographs of a 'casting expert' demonstrating the 'South African' side-swipe cast. They appeared in a very popular angling publication. The multiplier reel is mounted so low down on the rod that it would be an impossibility to obtain any 'fish-hauling' leverage if such a set of outlandish tackle was used for angling. However, as the casting court exponents are only concerned with getting out the lead to the maximum distance and not with reeling it back in again, plus perhaps a weighty fish – over snags and through weed – such problems never enter their heads as they nonchalantly wind back their weight over the billiards-table turf. To make this type of cast even more ludicrous; if applied to genuine shorefishing conditions, in the preparatory 'build-up' the weight is laid out on the smooth grass with almost a rod's length of line out, and then swished round at ground level and gradually raised as the rod begins to flex. While all these upper-body gyrations are going on, the caster's feet are performing some very neat weight-shift and foot-change manipulations which would do justice to an accomplished tango expert. You may like to try such suicidal antics if you own your own private mid-ocean desert island and it has a bowling-green type beach; otherwise concentrate on the sensible 'layback' style of casting which I am about to describe, and remain good friends with other beach users, and free from manslaughter charges!

Balancing Each Item of Tackle

The prime consideration for trouble-free, successful casting, is perfect balance between each separate item of tackle and also the suitability to the angler of the whole ensemble. He must be able to make it function properly, so that it reaches the limit of its casting distance potential. As the 'reverse taper' type of shorefishing rod is eminently suited to the layback style of casting, I would strongly recommend it as a 'first rod' because of its smooth, rather slow, easy action. This characteristic allows the beginner who is nervous and unsure

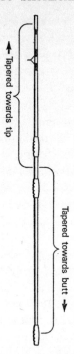

FIG. 15. Butt of a 'reverse-taper' rod

of himself, the greatest latitude for casting faults so far as a jerky build-up and a snatching forward release are concerned. As previously expounded in the chapter dealing with rods, their length, weight and distance from butt extremity to reel position is of major importance if a good, consistent casting style is to be cultivated. If you are shortish and below 5 feet 8 inches in height don't go for a heavy, lengthy pole over the 12-foot mark, as it is liable to tax your arm power severely and feel quite enormous and unwieldy when you go into action with it on the shoreline.

Reel positions, especially for multiplier users, are a critical factor which if wrong, can upset the whole casting performance. Generally, you will find that most ready-made, shop bought rods of the reverse taper design have their reel fittings set somewhere about the 38-in. mark – which is very unfortunate if it is fixed at that distance, because it may be quite unsuitable for the reach of the person who is buying the rod. The only way round this knotty problem is to fit a reel on the rod and test it personally. With feet apart and, if you are a right handed caster, left shoulder facing the direction of the cast, take the rod butt in the casting grip (left hand on the butt and right hand just beneath the reel, so that the thumb can rest comfortably on the spool), and see how it is for ease of operation.

Two important aspects of your hand positioning should be observed closely, as failure to rectify any trouble at this point will lead to untold mishaps on the shore. If your arms feel too stretched and extended, the reel should be moved down the rod an inch or two until a comfortable stance can be obtained. Failure to adjust this hand to hand distance, will result in the upper (right) hand unconsciously sliding down the rod to obtain a more comfortable grip whilst the cast is being made, so that when the time comes for a slowing-down thumb to be applied to check the reel spool, it will be out of reach farther down the rod, and a catastrophic 'overrun' will result. Conversely, if the reel position is too low, so that your hands are close together, you will not feel stretched so far as your arms are concerned; but when the casting motion is being made, the hands, which are too close, will tend to turn over the rod too rapidly. This will produce a jerk-and-snatch rod movement which will prove equally as disastrous as the thumb which was incapable of controlling the reel spool.

Reels – Use and Care
A word here on multiplier reels, their design, the loading of them with line, and the essential maintenance which will ensure faultless casting. Avoid at all costs, reels which do not have two spools and what is known in the tackle trade as 'one screw take-apart'. You will certainly save a couple of pounds in money by purchasing a reel with just the one spool which can only be extracted from the reel cage by the use of a screwdriver and the withdrawal of anywhere up to half a dozen rather small 'fiddly' screws. But your temper will be-

come frayed when you 'back-lash' and have to pack up fishing for the rest of the session, also every time you wish to give the reel a thorough cleaning and oiling. Two spools and the easy removal of either one of them in a second or two, by the simple operation of unscrewing a small knurled nut, simplifies the shorecaster's life immensely, and removes many frustrations. A two-spool, quick-change reel will enable you not only to have two different strengths of line instantly available, but it will brighten life considerably when that snarl-up in the dark does occur (and we all get them sooner or later), and you are able to drop out quickly the 'bundle of knitting', replace it with your spare spool and continue fishing immediately.

A great many shorecasters use what is known as a 'casting piece' or a 'shock leader' which is an extra-strong length of line (around 40 lb. b.s.) which is blood-knotted to the main reel line and withstands the extra 'power-drive' during the casting operation. There are a few distinct snags to their use and I personally do not like them. To be effective they should be slightly longer than two complete rod lengths, so that when the lead weight is attached and the casting position taken up, the whole of the line off the reel and half a dozen or so of the uppermost turns on it, consist of the special strong casting piece. One of my objections to such an arrangement is that right at the commencement of the cast, just after the reel thumb releases the spool, a rather jerky, unnerving blood-knot jumps up and jars along the rod through the whole of the rings. Furthermore, if you are fishing with such a strong bottom-end to your tackle over very snaggy ground, each time you have to 'pull-for-a-break' you are liable to lose the whole of your casting piece link as well as some of your weaker breaking strain main reel line. Therefore the strong casting piece technique completely precludes the use of the 'weak-link', reduced breaking strain, step-down terminal tackle arrangement. My last, and final point on the subject of 'shock-leaders' is that when fishing with one, on a shoreline where there is a strong lateral flow of tide and masses of floating weed, the joining knot, which is just about four or five yards above your terminal tackle, gathers up tremendous amounts of weed into a huge bunch and thereby effectively deadens any bite indications which may be telegraphed up the line from a taking fish. Also this annoying knot with its locked-on weed bunch frequently becomes jammed solid at the top rod ring and brings the whole reeling-in action to a full stop. This can be infuriating if you are about to beach a very good fish!

When you finally do decide upon a twin-spooled, one-screw-take-apart, multiplier reel and bear it home in triumph in its brand-new wrappings, for goodness sake do read the instruction booklet from cover to cover and give the line capacity chart and the lubrication instructions some considerable thought. As nylon monofil line has a powerful crushing effect if wound on to the reel spool under great tension, it is advisable to put on first a 'crush-cushion' of three or four thicknesses of some soft string or linen tape, before the actual fishing line is tied securely to the centre part of the spool and reeled on under slight tension in neat left-to-right, right-to-left 'cotton bobbin' style coils.

The oil you use on all reels is of great importance and it should never be of the unknown 'tool shed oilcan' variety which is liable to contain dirt and sludge, as well as grit, if it has been left standing for any length of time with the lid off. When you first begin casting with a brand-new reel, your style will most probably be very jerky, and I am quite sure that you will put lots of beef into it instead of letting the rod do the work. Without a doubt, the reel will run away with you so that an off-putting 'bird's nest' results. In difficult situations like this, the correct use of a rather thick motor oil will appreciably slow down the reel effectively if it is judiciously applied to the spool bearings or spindle mountings. If you find that you have drastically overdone this slowing-down treatment, and the oil you have used seems too thick, so that the reel gives a very sluggish performance, be not dismayed. Take the reel apart, and after flushing out all the oil from the works under a warm water tap, leave the reel and spool to dry out before the fire overnight on a sheet of newspaper. Then, when it is thoroughly dried out the next day, do a further experimental test with a slightly thinner oil until you strike the happy medium and the reel performs to perfection.

On reels with an adjustable end-play finger screw, the temptation to tighten it up and thereby use it as a spool-bearing restrictor (to cut down over-runs) is very great. Resist such inclinations as they can completely ruin the reel bearings by allowing them to operate under pressure, or even grind the bearings into the ball-races and wreck them. Alternatively, if the reel is a bearing-less, spindle and housing type, and it is screwed up tight by the adjusting screw, the spindles, by revolving at speed in their metal housing during casting, can generate so much heat that they seize up. The reel will then need a very expensive repair by the makers.

Without a doubt at some time or other, all shorefishers prepare to cast when using a multiplier reel; and thinking they have put the drum into 'free spool', by moving the disengage lever, they start the mighty sweep forward and are completely astounded when, as they release the reel spool, the rod continues to jerk forward, the line parts with a sharp crack, and the lead and terminal tackle does the 'double ton'. Unfortunately you are completely unattached. To safeguard yourself against this very unnerving happening (and cheat the shoreline observers who have a good laugh when this occurs) you should always carry out what is known as the 'drop down' technique. Simply explained; when you take up your layback casting position, sideways to the water with rod extended towards the shoreline; wind up the line so that the lead is a little too close to the rod end. Then, to make doubly sure you are in free-spool and have really disengaged the gears and operated that important little lever, ease your reel thumb up off the spool a little and allow about a foot of line to be pulled off the reel. You are now absolutely sure that you have operated the free-spool lever, and most important, that the mechanism is working correctly. It is surprising how often during casting that you almost let fly, and then at the eleventh hour test the reel with the 'drop down' precaution to find to your horror that the reel is still in gear.

A good tip when fishing in the dark and using the 'drop-down' technique to ensure a free-spool, is to tie on your main reel line to terminal tackle buckle-swivel attachment a little too short. You can then wind up your lead before casting until you feel the swivel come up against the rod tip ring, and after operating the free-spool lever, let just a bare six inches of line run off, so that you are sure that the line hanging from your rod end with the lead on it is just about the right length for a successful cast. This precaution saves you from having to wave your rod end around towards the Tilley lamp (if you are using one), to check that you have the correct length of 'dangle' from your rod end.

It is an acknowledged fact that narrow-drummed multiplier reels perform a better job of shorecasting than those with a great wide drum which house many more yards of line than can comfortably be cast. The reel with a narrow drum feeds off the nylon monofil to the rod rings in better alignment than a great wide drum with the line coming off in a criss-cross movement from one side to the other. A great amount of line capacity on a large, wide reel drum can also be a drawback to casting efficiency. At the commencement of the cast, on a reel drum which is narrow and does not hold too much line, the nylon comes off quite fast, but then as the reel drum empties down into the spool 'well', the amount of line released gets less and less. This is advantageous towards the end of the cast as the lead is slowing down and the line release also needs to be reduced. With a very wide, deep spool, a cast of one hundred yards hardly reduces the depth of line on the spool, so that the revolving drum is still throwing off almost the same amount of line at the end of the cast as it was at the beginning. To rectify this a very hard thumbing pressure is often needed early in the cast to smooth it out, and this cuts down distance.

The 'Moment of Truth'
At last, after many warnings, recommendations and casting tips, we are ready to face the great moment of truth as we take our brand new rod, reel, tackle and bait down to a

secluded shoreline to put into practise everything about shore-casting which is buzzing around like a swarm of angry bees in our heads. At this stage in your rod swishing career, spectators should be firmly discouraged, especially if they are idly curious and intent on a little light entertainment at your expense. The only companions or helpers I would tolerate on such a serious occasion, are extremely experienced casters who are patient and sympathetic; most decidedly not testy, irascible self-styled experts who have an abiding desire to grab the rod, push you out of the way with a sardonic snort and show you how it is done.

The most difficult part of the whole casting operation is to refrain from using uncoordinated brute strength, and by employing the very minimum of physical effort, let the rod do all the work. To attempt any kind of preconceived target distance in your initial casting stages is absolutely fatal to developing a good, sound, trouble-free technique. Your first casts should be no more than very gently, fully controlled swings of the rod, which allow the lead to proceed on its forward flight and be checked easily with a gentle pressure of the reel thumb on the spool. Wear a finger stall, a thin glove, or a piece of sticking plaster to prevent blisters at first.

Although, for all prospective shorecasters I would advocate a little practice on a deserted playing field, I certainly know how it feels to own a set of newly acquired fishing tackle and then be instructed to launch it on something so absolutely devoid of anything 'fishy' as a grass field. Therefore, by all means start your angling instruction in the appropriate en-vironment – on the edge of the rolling deep – if you are impatient to have a chance to come to grips (after you have landed it) with your first real live fish. By commencing your casting operations while using baited terminal tackle that wonderful, mysterious charm called beginner's luck may smile upon you, and that truly disappointing twenty-yard cast into quite shallow water may result most amazingly in a rod-tearing bite which jangles your nerves, but at the same time gives you the truly unforgettable experience of reeling in and landing your first fish!

So now, after swishing the rod around in a rather haphazard fashion and managing to get the lead out perhaps thirty or forty yards against a rather strong thumbing action (to prevent overruns), let us seriously approach the real distance-producing method of the layback cast. To adopt the correct casting position if you are right handed, you should stand sideways-on to the water with feet firmly planted just slightly wider apart than the width of your shoulders; left foot nearest the water and right foot away from it. The rod is held across the chest, left hand on the butt extremity grip, right hand gripping the upper part of the rod butt, just underneath the multiplier reel, so that the thumb comfortably hovers over the spool. The reel and rod rings should be pointing downwards and the rod should be extended shorewards, parallel to the ground; the right arm is almost fully extended and all your weight is on the back (right) foot.

At this point, use the drop-down check, by releasing the thumb a fraction to make sure everything is running free (very important in the dark), and begin the forward drive of your cast with about three or four feet of drop from tip ring to the lead. As the rod is swung up and over the right

FIG. 16. The three positions of the 'Layback' cast

shoulder (not vertically over the head), the right hand begins a steady forward drive and simultaneously the left hand starts to pull back (not jerkily) and down towards the left knee. At this stage, the balance of the whole body has been moved from the right foot forward on to the left, as the rod arcs in the forward power drive and the all-important thumb is released from the reel spool to let the actual cast commence. *Watch the lead* (I hope you will not be so foolish as to try to learn to cast in the dark) and allow that vital right thumb to hover very close to the reel spool, actually feeling the line running out without retarding it. That thumb is your life saver. It drops down instantly on to the spool when the lead hits the water and 'kills the reel' so that it does not throw off any more line. It is also your insurance against a jerky cast which starts off the development of a dreaded back-lash. Throughout the flight of the lead, if the slightest rattle or uneven line release is suspected, thumb firmly (this is the reason for the plaster, glove or finger stall), and drop the lead safely into the sea so that a snarl-up does not occur.

When reeling in, always lay on the line in even coils, and if you should get excited and reel in a good fish so that there is a big bump of line coiled in the middle of your reel spool – *be warned*. Do not try a cast until you have walked backwards along the shore, paying line off the reel and then spooled it back again in the approved even-coil manner.

So far as fixed-spool reels are concerned, which are mounted in approximately the same position as the multipliers. These are quite simple to cast with as they have no revolving drum to check and watch. Those remarks apply equally to side-cast reels which are usually mounted well down the rod, sometimes just a very short distance from the lower end of the butt.

Casting with Scarborough tackle is a very difficult art which few writers care to approach as they have had no experience of such formidable gear. Fortunately I grew up with such tackle and managed to overcome the hazards of skinned knuckles and break-off leads at a very early age. I would strongly advocate anyone who wishes to master the Scarborough casting style to seek out an expert exponent of it and just sit around and watch him, preferably on a high cliff top on a glorious summer's day for maximum pleasure. It is this 'back to the sea' start which scares off most Scarborough tackle beginners, especially if there is a very steep drop of about a hundred feet below and the wind is blowing strongly offshore.

To cut out all risk of over-balancing should a very disastrous lash-up occur which jerks the caster momentarily forward, I strongly recommend a safe, harbour wall stance on firm, dry stone a yard or so back from the edge. A fairly long drop of line from rod tip to lead is needed to get the correct back-swing for the half circle swivel which is the Scarborough cast power drive. But in your early stages it is most wise to practise a very gentle swing and get used to controlling the reel spool, so that it is having the line pulled from it by the lead, rather than accelerating and *throwing* off coils which invariably brings the dreaded 'birds-nest'.

Practising with Scarborough gear from a high, but safe casting stance a gentle lob will put the lead quite a considerable distance without a great deal of power being used, and while making these gentle swings, control of the reel can be mastered before the really beefy powerhouse style of casting is attempted from rough, rocky shores or towering cliffs.

CHAPTER ELEVEN

The Shorecaster's Fishes

Each Wednesday, as I emerge slowly from my newsagent's shop after buying the two angling newspapers which I read from cover to cover, I am apt either to stumble down the steps, or bump into other customers who are entering the premises; because I just cannot rid myself of the shocking habit of having a quick peep through the papers to see what new and almost unbelievable shore catches have been made in the preceding week.

This one aspect of the glorious uncertainty of sea fishing is a most fascinating part of it and cannot be matched by any branch of freshwater angling in totally enclosed lakes or ponds. When freshwater fishing it is only possible to take out (probably in greatly increased sizes) those species which you know are there by natural development or have been put in by planned re-stocking, so that there is seldom a genuine 'unknown quantity' involved in your fishing.

In sharp contrast to the size and shallow depth of the average coarse fishery; as I stand on the tideline with rod in hand – especially on a bright moonlit night when all the water surface seems alive – I constantly allow my thoughts to wander and speculate upon the vastness of the oceans, which though far distant, are all connected parts of the small area which I am fishing. In such circumstances my mind is inclined to conjure up great and very rare fish which could just happen to stray far from their natural locations and sample my bait. Lest anyone should accuse me of senseless day-dreaming, I would, in defence of my romantic theories, advise them to keep a very close watch on the newspaper columns at seaside towns throughout a hot summer. It is amazing how many unusual captures are made in the nets of inshore commercial fishermen. One aspect of the situation which has me living in constant trepidation during very warm weather, is the number of sharks which are to be found quite close inshore. At such times when tens of thousands of carefree holiday maker's legs are dangling (temptingly to a shark, if one should be cruising around) just below the surface of the water as they sport about in the briny!

Having digressed a little and strayed into the realms of big game fish and the mysterious leviathans, about which we really known very little, let us now make a detailed survey of what can be caught around our shores with rod and line from the various types of fishing station. Also of utmost importance, we must begin by making a division in the ranks of both the anglers and the fish they catch, for reasons which are most significant ethically, and also from a fish conservation viewpoint.

Some anglers (and happily the number is increasing) have very high principles so far as their catch is concerned, and strictly limit their methods to the taking of those species which are generally accepted in this country as table fish. In addition, they kill only such a quantity as they themselves can eat fresh, or store for their own personal use in the family deep freezer. To witness what I will call 'mackerel slaughter time' at a seaside resort in the height of summer is a very enlightening insight into human frailty of the worst possible kind. A distressing lust to kill seems to overcome some members of the angling fraternity on occasions when the mackerel shoals are close inshore and the fish are absolutely suicidal in their frenzied efforts to get themselves caught.

Is it any wonder therefore, that certain outspoken members of the non-angling public who are taking a holiday stroll along the harbour wall, condemn all forms of fishing as wanton blood sport. Eyes and nostrils are assailed by the sight (and smell) of a huge pile of sun-scorched fish heaped behind a rod-flailing maniac whose sole aim in life seems to be to transfer as many of the shoaling mackerel as he possibly can, at great speed, from their natural habitat, the sea, on to the stones behind him. Then with an unbelievable non-chalance, calmly walks away, leaving the lot to go rotten or be cleared up by some poor, unfortunate garbage disposal operator!

Non-food Fish

Lest anyone should think I am knocking all shorecasters, and whilst on this very delicate subject of fish conservation, the lamentable lack of which is constantly getting fishing a bad name, let me acquaint my readers with the obligations which are incumbent upon all anglers (shore and boat) who choose to concentrate their activities on the various species of fish (usually of a large and embarrassing size) which are not generally accepted as food fish. From a publicity and personal ego point of view, it is very gratifying to be photographed with rod 'at the high port' and yards of fish slung up from a boat's mast or harbourside girder, complete with chalked board which plainly states (in weight – will it be pounds or kilos?) what a marvellously successful angler you are! However, when the shouting has died down, the cameramen have departed and the corpse is lowered and lies in a flaccid heap at your feet – how do you dispose of it? That question should be considered and the right answers found before you actually set out to catch such a fish. It is much too late once you have landed it, and banged it on the head in order to unhook it, and then left it to expire on the deck of a boat or on the shoreline.

A number of large, non-food fish (mostly of the shark family) can be taken by shorecasters from quite shallow water, especially during hot summer weather, when they move close in to rocky headlands and up muddy estuaries and creeks in order to forage around. It behoves the shorefisher who seeks to obtain sport from them to decide well in advance how he is going to deal with the catch when he has hooked and landed it. My personal views on the matter are that they should be unhooked by the most humane method possible and returned to the water immediately. If they are killed, they should be disposed of by the angler and not indiscriminately dumped under cover of darkness out of sight behind some harbour wall, or left drifting around on the tideline. Such bloated, objectionable eyesores do very little towards improving our image in the eyes of people who are antagonistic to our sport.

Humane Killing

While on this rather 'tender' subject of killing your catch quickly, humanely and in a completely dispassionate manner when onlookers may be present. Let me give some sound advice which could save angry scenes if you are surrounded by over-sentimental adults with children, who would rather take the squeamish line of letting a fish slowly gasp out its life; than have it despatched quickly.

Equip yourself in the early stages of your shorecasting career with a 'quietener', in the form of an 18 in. length of iron piping, in which about ½ lb. of molten lead has been poured, at one end, to produce a 'loaded cosh'. The opposite end to the weighted one should be bound with rough cord or encased in a cycle 'handle-bar-grip', stuck on firmly, to provide a secure non-slip finger hold, especially if you are liable to use it with wet, slimy hands.

With this very lethal, 'blunt-instrument' almost all of the fish which you are liable to encounter from the shoreline can be killed instantly. Immediately they have been unhooked (if required for eating) give them a couple of short, sharp and well aimed blows over the head right between the eyes, while holding them firmly, in position on the beach, rocks, pier-planking or concrete with your free hand.

Conger eels and certain smaller members of the shark family present more difficulty. They may lie very still and seemingly dead for hours on end after having had the 'iron-pipe' treatment. Then, quite suddenly, they come alive and either attack their unsuspecting captors or leap back into the sea and rapidly swim away out of sight, apparently none the worse for wear, despite a heavy pounding around the head.

Treat such fish with extreme care and never ever presume them dead until you are absolutely sure that they are. Failure to take such precautions could cost you lost fingers or toes!

Congers can be momentarily subdued by giving them a heavy blow in the 'lymph heart' region – below their vent at the tail end. The shark species will also quieten down for a while after a few heavy blows on the snout. To kill all fish cleanly and in a manner which is not messy, a very sharp knife with a one-piece, rigid blade and handle (not hinged – it may fold up on your fingers) should be driven cleanly through the vertebrae just behind the head, immediately after the subduing treatment has been administered.

If you are foolish enough to give a sadistic display of fish head 'bashing', before a crowd of holiday makers, you can expect some very adverse comments. However if you quietly turn your back on any onlookers, administer your 'last rites' with speed and efficiency and then stow the corpse away in your fish bag, very little will be seen of what is always a most controversial action to those who do not understand the angling scene.

Flatfish
Of all the fish we are liable to take from the shoreline, I am quite sure that the four popular species commonly referred

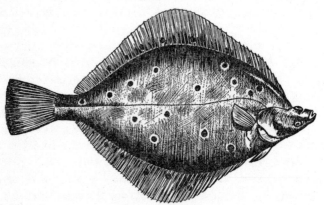

FIG. 17. Plaice

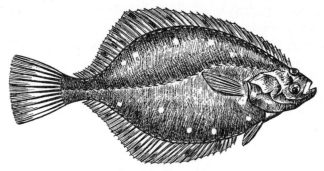

Fig. 18. Flounder

to loosely as 'flatties' (plaice, flounders, sole and dabs) are
the most accommodating. They are widely distributed around
our coast, and from a frying-pan and hot fat aspect, most
desirable when reclining crisp and browned on a bed of golden
chips! I think the reason why the flatfish category of shorefishing has over the years become so maligned, is the outlandishly heavy tackle which has been employed to take them.
A great stout pole, thick lines, a heavy lead, and a 'Christmas
tree' style terminal tackle rig of six hooks may ensure that
they are winched in at intervals by the half dozen; but such a
method cannot sincerely be classed as shorefishing. It really
smacks of a miniature version of the commercial type of
'long-line'.

The most satisfying way to take flounders, plaice, sole and
dabs, is by angling for them with the very lightest of tackle
which the conditions will allow. They are usually to be found
over what is termed as a 'kindly' bottom (of mud, sand,
shingle or mussel and worm beds), where a gentle run of tide
allows the use of just an ounce or two of lead, and the lightest
of beachcasters or even a coarse fishing carp or pike rod will
allow them to show their mettle, especially if a line of about
7–8 lb. is used in conjunction with either a fixed-spool reel or
a small multiplier.

This quartet of flatfish are not fussy feeders so far as bait
is concerned. They will take marine worms, and for the
flounder, earthworms as well, fished with a small, long-

shanked hook (about sea size 1/0 or 2/0 or smaller, down into the freshwater scale) on a flowing trace so that they can thoroughly fuss over and investigate the bait without feeling any direct resistance, of which they seem to become highly suspicious. When fishing over areas where there are worm or shellfish beds, the bait situation almost resolves itself. The angler arrives at dead low water and after helping himself to a generous bait box of whatever is going free (mussels, cockles, razor fish, lug or ragworm), he then fishes this bait (usually with great success) over the same ground on which he collected it – his method which ensures that the hook offering is appropriately identical to that type of food which the fish are seeking.

An explanatory word on the habits and foibles of this 'fishy foursome' will enable you to pursue them at the best time of day or night with a suitable bait; when the weather and the season are most favourable to the taking of them. Plaice have bright orange spots and grow to well over the ten pound mark, but the largest taken on rod and line from boats over deep water have been near to eight pounds. From the shore, if you latch on to one of half that weight you will certainly make angling news and have a glorious feed of fillets. The disappointing habit which plaice suffer from, so far as the shorefisher is concerned, is their yearning for deep water when they begin to grow over the pound mark; so that the shorefisher's loss is the boat angler's gain. In complete reverse, that great traveller the flounder, swims everywhere and fins its way miles up rivers where it then allows itself to be caught by amazed coarse fish anglers using maggots, worms and even

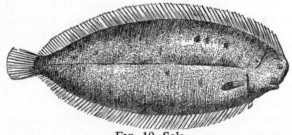

FIG. 19. Sole

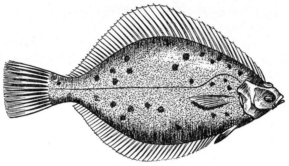

FIG. 20. Dab

bread on float tackle. Five pounds is a record flounder, three or four pounders are the very elder brethren, and two pounders come fairly regularly from good flounder marks. Flounders move out to sea to spawn in the late months of winter and early spring somewhere around December to March, as also do the plaice.

The 'night-owl' shorecasters who fish throughout the hours of darkness in summer over sandy bays and estuarial mud-flats are most likely to take that nocturnal feeder the oval-shaped sole. This fish is of great culinary value, but alas, as with all good things, it only reaches a top weight of about 4 lb. and moves out into deep water to winter in comparative peace and safety.

Cod

Let us leave the ubiquitous flatfish and move on into the ranks of the 'round fish' and consider that great money-spinner of the fish and chip shops and also the most important commercial fish-dish, the cod; in all its capacious, coal-scuttle-mouthed glory! It is a fish of cold waters and therefore it will be found in its greatest numbers around our northern coastline, down the east North Sea shoreline, and part of the way along the south coast, petering out as we near the west country areas of Devon and journey round the Cornish coast. Shorecasting newcomers are apt to become bewildered by the terms 'cod' which they know are those big headed, bearded fish which grace the fishmonger's slab and 'codling', the fish which the Yorkshire coast anglers seek so avidly in foul, wintry weather. To clarify this puzzling question of terminology, I would say that the diminutive addition of 'ling' can be tacked on to the name cod when the fish concerned is in the bantam-weight category and takes the spring balance down to 5–6 lb. or less.

Cod (or alternatively codling) fishing is primarily a winter game. It attracts a very hardy breed of anglers who, as they emerge from cars and other well equipped travelling kitchen-cum-dormitories, wander off shorewards with rods and bait boxes, often in thick snow or driving rain, are viewed with frank amazement by shivering, scurrying non-anglers, who find it hard to believe that anyone could presume to take their pleasures out in such weather. Late September and early October should see the cod arriving; but a really warm autumn and early winter can delay their appearance for weeks – even months – so that some years, very few cod arrive to bring joy to the brigades of 'Tilley lamp' shore anglers until the new year, and at times, for no apparent reason, a completely blank run of cod seasons is suffered on some parts of the coast for perhaps two or three consecutive winters. Anglers are then driven almost to distraction and begin to think that their favourite quarry have completely deserted them – and usually just about then old *Gadus morhua* (to give it its Latin name) comes swimming in strongly through the breakers on a good rough onshore blow, and puts the sparkle back into their eyes once more as they take their cod-poles, multipliers and oilskins out of mothballs!

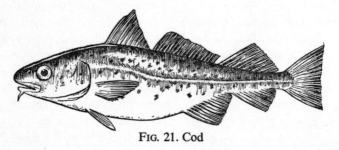

FIG. 21. Cod

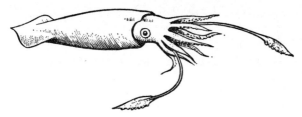

FIG. 22. Small whole squid

I think the greatest attraction of the cod to shorecasters is the glorious uncertainty of what size your catch could be. Ranging from a string of two dozen one- to two-pounders (which make glorious eating if gutted, head-and-tailed and fried in deep fat with the bone in to give added flavour), right up to the twenty-, thirty- and even near-forty-pounders – just a few of which have been landed by shorefishers; amazingly in the last year or two.

Baits are no problem if enough is available, but certain localities have their favourite hook offerings which seem to work best, and it is wise, if you intend to become a journeyman angler, to refrain from having very fixed, inflexible ideas on all aspects of tackle, technique, presentation and hook offerings.

Lugworm seems to be the popular standard bait for shore codding as it is most convenient to obtain it via the tackle shops in those flat gory-looking newspaper parcels which are supposed to contain fifty worms but alas, they have a most consistent failing of being rather short – some diggers seem to suffer a complete mental block when the figure of thirty-five is reached! Razor fish, hermit and peeler crabs, sprats, herring strip, ragworm, mussels and small whole squid will all tempt cod if used at the right fishing stations. For the really big tackle-testers a very ingenious method of natural livebaiting has proved successful. Briefly; a small baited hook is mounted on the terminal tackle just above a much larger hook which remains bare; the idea being that when a small fish takes the bait and becomes hooked, it is not reeled in by the angler, but the tackle is left out in order that a foraging cod of immense proportions may swim along and seize the small fish struggling on the hook. Then, when the angler strikes at the bite, the bigger fish becomes impaled on the large hook which was incorporated into the tackle set-up for just that purpose.

Bass

If the flatfish provide the shorecaster with a fairly easily caught, widely distributed quarry, and the cod (or codling) afford him a cold weather catch which can run into stones or even hundredweights (with many choice fillets and fish and chip suppers) – the bass – that enigmatic, spiky dorsal finned aristocrat of the saltwater shorecasting scene – will give him anything else which he finds lacking in the other two. Bass enthusiasts, who fish for nothing else, disappear shorewards in the gathering gloom to stand out all alone, waist deep in surf in the dark. By the pale light of dawn they appear with a strange gleam in their eye and perhaps just one four- or five-pounder in their bag, which they have allowed themselves to keep, out of perhaps a dozen others; all unhooked and returned to grow bigger. Need I say more about their dedication? It can only be fully understood by fellow bass anglers!

Please disregard any angling literature in which the bass is described as a 'southern half of the country' fish – one which inhabits only the inshore waters of the south-east, south and south-west coasts. The bass is most certainly found in varying

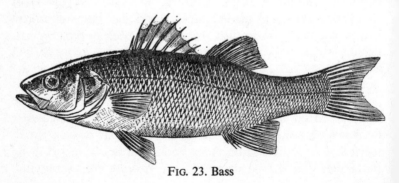

FIG. 23. Bass

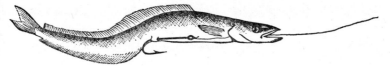

FIG. 24. Live sand eel on hook

concentrations all around the shores of Great Britain. It is anglers to take them who are few and far between in certain districts, so that although the fish are themselves present, reports of them are not publicised because the bass are not being angled for! To give just two instances of which I have personal knowledge. Off the Yorkshire beaches, and especially in the Spurn Peninsular area, quite a few shorecaught bass, right up to low double figures, are taken every summer and well into the autumn by shorefishers who do not read the angling press and who have no desire to have their favourite beach marks noised abroad so that they quickly become crowded. Again, up there on the west coast of Scotland (Luce Bay to be precise) some angling friends of mine 'discovered' that bass could be caught there around the period May to October, and they took their first fish way back in the mid 1960s.

Don't expect to connect with a record-breaking bass of around 18 lb. as they are about as scarce as a win on the football pools. However, the lesser of the species in the 1–3 lb. range (called 'schoolies'), and one or two much heavier may certainly fall to a very lightly leaded terminal tackle fished with a 'soft-crab' bait on a fine wired hook, or a small live sandeel or pouting suspended beneath float tackle cast from a rock mark into lively, well oxygenated water.

The Thornback Ray

Time now to consider that rather ugly, slime-coated, hand-lacerating creature of the summer-warmed shallow waters; the thornback ray. A brute to deal with and prepare for the table, but an unrivalled gastronomic dream of pink fleshed delight, when the fearsome task of 'wrassling' the 'wings' and the tough leathery skin apart has been accomplished, and the corrugated flesh has been fried in the deep, hot fat of a large chip-basket pan.

Thornbacks (or 'roker' as they are called along the east coast) come right inshore at quite a number of places all around our coast, especially in areas where there are gently shelving sandy beaches and estuary mud-flats interspersed with sand, gravel and shell patches to provide these bottom-hovering 'crab crunchers' with a mixed diet of crustacea and live fish such as small flatfish or sandeels, not to mention the rich pickings of lugworm from the mud. I am sure that their main object in entering the sun-warmed shallows, especially at night when thornback fishing is at its best, is to do a little comfortable, uninterrupted courting. Each female seems to have a retinue of male followers, judging by the way in which a predominance of male rays are taken.

Armchair beach snoozers will enjoy thornback fishing on warm summer nights. There is no real need for a 'rush up and grab the rod' technique to be practised, as the ray needs plenty of time to investigate and finally take the bait. Fairly light tackle can be used as these fish are not really spirited fighters. Apart from a few fluttering 'kites' up and down off

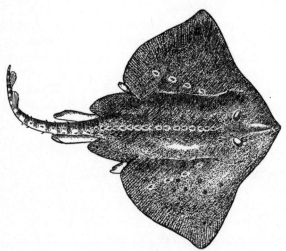

FIG. 25. Thornback ray

the bottom, they tend to sulk most of the time, and in very shallow water dig their noses into the sand when being reeled in the last few yards. Although a main reel line somewhere in the region of 15–20 lb. can be used in conjunction with a very light lead of say 2–3 oz. on beaches where there is very little tidal flow; because of the crunching, grinding ability of the thornback's dentistry, a heavy nylon monofil hook length needs to be used. For greater safety use a rather soft, pliable wire trace with a very sharp, long shanked hook of an appropriate size to mount the bait which could be crab, worm, a bunch of live shrimps, a small flatfish, lug or rag-worm and shellfish 'cocktail', squid or fish strip. Try them all – feeding rays will accept a wide variety of offerings.

The most enjoyable way I know to fish for thornbacks is to place the rod in a good monopod and use a multiplier reel which has the lightest of 'tru-play' settings on it and then, settling back comfortably in your beach lounger chair, watch the rod tip, or alternatively close your eyes and rely on your ears telling you when the line is trickling out by the steady metallic 'clicking' of the reel as the handle slowly turns. To observe a rod when a ray is sampling the bait is a thrilling sight. Instead of a 'tip-rattle', the whole rod from tip to butt gently undulates and dithers as the thornback hovers over, and eventually flops on to, the bait. Then it shuffles around until its mouth finally locates the hook offering. Next it commences to grind away at it before finally engulfing the lot and flapping away, which is the precise time to pick up the rod and, as the fish tightens the line, lean back into a good

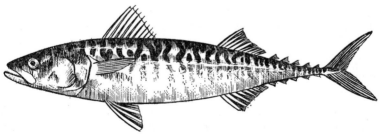

FIG. 26. Mackerel

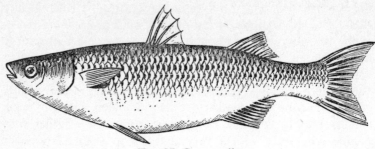

FIG. 27. Grey mullet

sweeping strike to set the hook. The record thornback ray is 38 lb. but an exceptional beach-caught fish will not weigh much above 10–12 lb. The best eating size are those in the 4–5 lb. region. The bigger they get the stronger they seem to taste.

Having once mentioned the mackerel when I made some derogatory remarks about certain thoughtless anglers who slaughter dozens of them, I will not dwell upon them long, but will merely express the view that during the summer months when they shoal and can be caught from the shore, they can provide superb sport if they are angled for with the lightest of tackle and a single baited hook fished under a float, or a small lure or spinner, so that just one fish is taken. When considering fish which can be angled for with light gear, the mullet must take pride of place over all the other shore fisher's quarry as the one which demands a specialist approach, since very few will be caught by accident while angling for other species. The mullet is primarily a fish of the south and south-west coast, where it roams the harbours, tidal creeks and estuaries. To watch the Cornish mullet experts at work is indeed an education. Coarse fishermen, who are sampling sea fishing for the first time, would do well before they launch out on a tackle buying spree, to consider what gear they already own can be adapted to their new branch of angling, as the wily mullet is one species which can best be taken with coarse fishing tackle, and the stealth of approach normally employed by specimen chub or carp catchers.

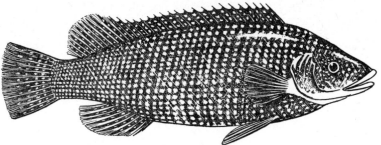

FIG. 28. Ballan wrasse

Mackerel, Wrasse and Lesser Species

Wrasse fishing is another specialist branch of shorecasting which usually demands that the angler is first possessed of a good rock-climbing technique and equipment. The favourite haunts of the three most common species of the wrasse (ballan, cuckoo, and corkwing) are those rather dangerous and lonely rock marks which give on to deep water with profuse bottom weed and deep crevasses where, with great square, protruding front teeth these fish calmly crunch up shellfish and crabs. On such baits, fished beneath float tackle to avoid the snaggy bottom, wrasse can be taken on the hottest and calmest of days when little else is moving or showing the slightest interest in an angler's bait.

To conclude the lesser species of the shorecaster's quarry, before I go on to describe some of the larger (but often not very palatable) rod benders. There is a tiro of what some discerning anglers call 'nuisance' fish namely, the whiting, pouting and coalfish (or billet), which may sometimes be so

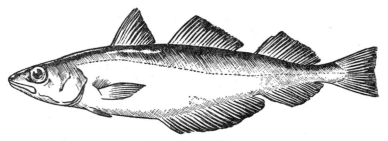

FIG. 29. Whiting

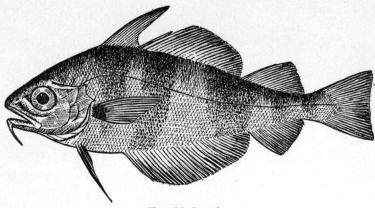

FIG. 30. Pouting

numerous in their smaller sizes as to constitute a bait-stealing pest. Diminutive whiting are at times the cod fisher's curse, as they readily accept his choice offering of bait instead of something more weighty in the shape of a double figure cod, to which family the 'poor relation' whiting does actually belong. As the whiting appears inshore during the winter months, which coincides with the appearance of the cod, they are most certainly infuriating when they hang themselves on to your hook when the cod are about; but a blessing in disguise if for some indefinable reason the cod fail to show, you can still take home a sizeable catch of whiting in the 2 lb. class and safeguard your reputation as a fresh fish provider!

If tiny pouting are the downfall and despair of southern anglers seeking larger, nobler quarry; then I am sure that the

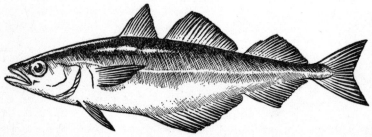

FIG. 31. Coalfish

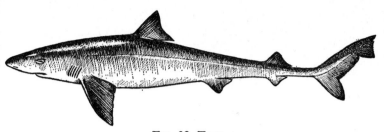

FIG. 32. Tope

huge shoals of small bait-gobbling coalfish (or billet) which
bedevil the anglers 'up north' are equally as off-putting. A
point which I must raise here, which I am sure is baffling to
all newcomers to sea angling. 'How is it,' they ask, 'that
you curse the tiny bait-stealing coalfish and say they are a
menace to the shorecaster, when in fact they are known to
grow to about 30 lb. and there are still bigger ones to be
taken.' This question can only be answered by revealing one
of the sad aspects of shorecasting, which is, that quite a
number of fish spend their infancy in very shallow water
and then move out to the deeps where they attain a much
greater size but seldom return within casting range of the
shorefisher for the rest of their lives.

Tope, dogfish and smooth-hounds are all members of the
shark family and can often be caught from the shore, sometimes in surprising numbers, usually in the summer months.
But of late our very mild 'sub-tropical' winters with very
little snow or frost, have enabled certain enthusiastic shorecasters to prove beyond doubt that the supposed migration to
deep, offshore waters by what are considered 'southern' warm-
water species is an archaic fallacy. These three species of
mini-shark are all recognised fish eaters and they can be taken

FIG. 33. Lesser spotted dogfish

F

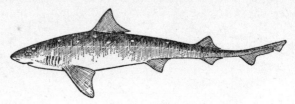

FIG. 34. Smooth hound

on the oily, fish strip 'sides' of mackerel, pilchard and herring, as well as fresh flatfish fillets. The dogfish and the tope favour a clean bottom of sand, gravel or shell; but the smooth-hound forages up muddy creeks and estuaries and can be taken in quite shallow water.

The tope is the real heavyweight as it can weigh up to around 70 lb., and at such a weight will quickly strip two or three hundred yards of line off your multiplier reel on its first run before it stops to chew the bait a little more before swallowing it. Top weight for smooth-hounds is about 28 lb., Greater Spotted Dogfish (or Bull Huss – beloved of the London area fish fryers) about 20 lb.; Lesser Spotted Dogfish 10 lb.; and Spurdog (the curse of commercial fishermen) 17 lb.

The Conger Eel
To conclude this chapter on some common fish which the shorecaster is most liable to hook, we will now approach in print the real 'rod-and-scale-buster' of them all and consider that formidable opponent, the conger eel. This creature is known sometimes to approach the weight of up to 200 lb., and has actually been caught on rod and line from a boat over a deep sea wreck at weights approaching and exceeding the 90 lb. mark. Some piers, harbour walls and rock marks have one or two resident conger, often of formidable proportions, which are frequently hooked (especially at night) by anglers fishing with normal shorecasting tackle and large fish baits or pieces of squid. Needless to say, the conger invariably takes the angler completely by surprise when he strikes at a runaway bite and finds himself hooked up to an immovable force which very quickly breaks his twenty-pound-plus line

FIG. 35. Conger

like cotton, or saws quite easily, with razor sharp teeth, through his hook snood. At the end of my next chapter, which deals with tackles, methods and baits for different fish at a variety of locations, I shall make special mention of some suitable tackle (which may seem outlandishly powerful) for successfully hauling out from its rocky lair the fish which has the honour of being able to give battle both before and also after being landed, or worse still brought into a small boat!

CHAPTER TWELVE

Tackles, Methods and Baits for Different Locations

In this final, rather lengthy chapter it is my intention to cover thoroughly in detail a whole succession of shorecasting angling situations and locations where the fisherman may meet a very wide variety of conditions so far as his casting stance, personal safety and underfoot mobility are concerned. I shall also discuss the tackle he must employ to beat the tidal flow (if it is exceptionally powerful) and the bottom (if it is weedy and snaggy). In addition to the correct tackle, personal apparel, footwear, illumination (if fishing at night), and rod holding or resting equipment, the bait must be right; and finally, if fishing over mud-flats, the angler's tackle bag and 'creature comforts' must be kept safe and dry. Rather a tall order to put into cold print. Nevertheless, after many years of hard-won experience down on the tideline, I am sure I can offer a lot of useful 'inside' information which will do a great deal to smooth the path of the shorecasting newcomer, so that he immediately feels confident, safe and at ease, thereby ensuring that he can concentrate on his fishing and not have a whole host of nagging doubts gnawing away in his mind and completely destroying his concentration.

Tackle

I am sure that by far the most common shorecasting situation is that to be met on a fairly steep shelving beach, which has a strong run of tide, and where it is necessary to employ what I would call heavy beachcasting tackle in order to put the terminal gear and bait out to where the fish are feeding. Bearing in mind also that the lead must be sufficiently heavy and of the right design to 'hold out' without rolling downtide and snagging the gear of other anglers (otherwise you will be most unpopular!) the rod and line must be of sufficient power and breaking strain to stand the casting of the necessary weight of lead. In addition to which the rod must be able to hit the fish and hook it at perhaps a hundred yards and then, in conjunction with the reel, bring both fish and trailing lead, and perhaps a goodly bunch of floating weed, in through a fast lateral-flowing tide. Quite a formidable task and one which will immediately show up any faults in your tackle if you err on the wrong side and sacrifice strength for ultra-lightness.

To beat the surf and hold the tackle steady, a 12 or 13 ft. 'Beachcaster' mounted in a firm-standing monopod which elevates the line above the breaking wave tops is vital. The multiplier reel needs to be of rugged construction and capable of taking at least two hundred yards of 25–30 lb. line on the spool without overfilling. Leads can be of the 5 or 6 oz. torpedo type with soft 3 or 4 in. wires. Or, if your funds run to them, the new 'Breakaway' type leads which are excellent, because they allow a lighter line to be used. They remove the irksome chore of reeling in across a soft sandy bottom a lead which has its wires bent into the anchor position so that it acts like a plough on the retrieve and puts a great amount of tension on the line, not to mention the fact that it 'holds back' when you are reeling in a fish which is skulking on the bottom assisted by the trailing lead.

As strong lateral tides, a lively surf, and thick, coloured water, usually mean that the fish are hunting their feed by scent rather than sight; big 'smelly' baits on large hooks with short, tangle-free snoods must all be incorporated into this 'strong flow', deep-water technique to ensure that it is most effective. This is the type of fishing which takes big cod and really outsize bass – those once-in-a-lifetime fish which are all too often hooked and lost because the tackle being used is sporty and only adequate for dealing with fish up to the 10 lb. range and not those rareties approaching 20 lb.!

A lighter, and much pleasanter method of surfcasting can be done during the gentle flow of neap tides, or from shore marks where there is no powerful lateral tidal flow, which allow a scaling down of tackle so that the fish are not hampered in their fight by a great weighty chunk of lead. This is the type of shorecasting where a single leg monopod or tripod rod-rest is quite unnecessary. The rod can be hand-held and the line gently tightened to a 1 oz., 2 oz. or at the very most, 3 oz. lead, so that the slightest shifting, slackening or tensioning of the line is transmitted up the rod to the hands of the angler. With a lot of practice, while fishing with such a shorecasting rig, very delicate 'takes' can be sensed rather than actually felt physically.

FIG. 36. Simple terminal tackle for bass

The rod can be one of those popularly described in the tackle catalogues as a 'bass rod' – about 11 ft. 6 in. long and designed to cast 1–3oz. which it will do comfortably to distances of up to 150 yards if used in conjunction with a precision multiplier with a narrow-drummed, plastic or nylon spool and a good quality nylon monofil line of about 15 lb. b.s. The ideal lead for this type of fishing is the swivelled 'Arlesey Bomb' which can be threaded on to the reel line and stopped by tying a plain double-eyed barrel swivel at the end through one link, and attaching a flowing trace of slightly lower breaking strain line to the other. At the end is mounted a hook of a suitable size to mount the bait which could, if the ground is fairly rough and interspersed with flat slabs of weed-covered rock, be ideally soft crab; or over patches of mud, sand or shell, one of the marine worm baits.

Small live fish can be a most deadly offering on this light tackle if they are hooked about twice through the root of the tail and secured additionally by a loop of fine thread passed

Fig. 37. Attaching live fish bait to hook

right through the eye of the hook, around the 'wrist' of the tail and tied off securely to the hook trace. The offering of small live or dead (but very fresh) fish on a lightly leaded flowing trace of either monofil, or alternatively wire, for those fish with formidable dentition and members of the shark family, which have rough abrasive skins, is one very sure method of sorting out the rod-benders of a wide variety of species. The biggest bass, cod, tope, skate, dogfish, smooth-hounds, conger, and very occasionally that rare but welcome 'chef's delight' the shore-caught turbot, will all fall for a 'cannibal' meal.

Deepwater- Fishing

Rock fishing into deep water is at times unbelievably pro-ductive and usually very exhilarating; but to strike a sobering note, it invariably has dangers which must not, for one single moment, ever be disregarded, or treated with foolish abandon. The successful rock fisher must also live in the area, so that he can constantly study the tides, the wind, the waves the weather – and above all, the approaches to the fishing plat-forms or vantage points. This is especially valuable if the paths lie over loose shale cliff walks or down sploshy clay, which dries out during periods of strong winds with no rain, but becomes a veritable man-trap quagmire after a prolonged deluge.

According to the nature of the bottom, a very great variety of fish can be taken from rock fishing stations, especially if the marks give on to very deep water, which more or less puts

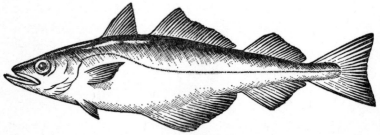

FIG. 38. Pollack

the rock fisher in the very enviable position of being able to fish into water quite as deep as that which in other circumstances would necessitate the use of a boat in order to get far enough offshore. He also avoids the ever present boatfisher's need to keep a constant watch on the weather in case it should rapidly deteriorate, necessitating a very quick up-anchor and a 'full-throttle' run for home.

Deep water rock marks can at times produce a really startling variety of fish species which are not usually considered to be the acknowledged shorecaster's quarry. Pollack, that power-diving lover of deep water pinnacle rock marks can be taken from rocky shores, but usually only in the smaller sizes around the 4–5 lb. mark. However, as the boat-caught record runs as high as 25 lb. there is always hope (in my optimistic mind at least), that a real tackle-testing pollack of well into double figures will one day be taken from some obscure Scottish shore rock mark and set the whole shorefishing world agog and reaching for its rod, rucksacks and climbing gear!

For heavy 'ground' or bottom fishing from rocks into deep water, I favour a Beachcaster rod which will throw a 6 oz. lead and a half-herring bait fifty or sixty yards; but the very long butted reverse-taper rods with 30 or 40 in. of projection below the reel fitting are most decidedly an accident-prone piece of equipment on anything but very smooth rock platforms. If a rod of the reverse-taper kind is being designated for rock fishing, a wise precaution would be to crop the 'bottom-hamper' a little by cutting off at least 12 in. to remove that foot-tangling portion which projects below the knees and does its level best to trip you up should you be dancing around in great excitement while playing a lively thirty-pound conger or tope from a rough, dodgy rock mark in the pitch blackness of a moonless night!

Float fishing from rock platforms into deep water in fairly calm weather can be the most delightful of shorecasting experiences, especially if the breeze is warm, the sun shining and the sea alive with shoaling mackerel or, on the Cornish coast, that magical fish, the mullet. This is where the coarse

FIG. 39. Cork-bodied 'Trotting' float

fisherman who has taken up shorecasting should be in his element, with appropriate tackle to match. Those 'specimen hunter' rods and high quality fixed-spool reels for carp, barbel, pike and heavy chub fishing can be made to do stirling work on the saltwater scene, provided they are feather bedded by a daily ritual of fresh water washing, cleaning and oiling after every excursion.

Lines around 10 lb. b.s. with pike floats or even very large cork-bodied 'trotting' floats, should be suitable, and they can be weighted down with a variety of leads such as swanshot, resin-cored solder chopped into 2–3 in. pieces and poked clear with stiff wire. For a heavier float and a lead to give weight for long casting what is known as a 'Jardine' spiral can be used. This style of light sea fishing with a bait temptingly suspended from a float to waft back and forth with the currents just above the bottom, or over the thick beds of weed, will account for a variety of sea fish which may include

FIG. 40. 'Jardine' spiral lead

wrasse, pollack, coalfish, mackerel, mullet, and where the ground is exceptionally rough, some really good bass, especially if a small pouting or live sandeel lip-hooked bait is used.

A very ingenious and most natural hook offering for the predatory bass which haunt rock marks, is the free-lined 'floating' fish method. A small pouting, mackerel or sprat is inflated by a hypodermic syringe, or made to float by pushing down its innards a small amount of polystyrene or the blown-up end portion of a sausage-shaped balloon. By varying the amount of inflation of the floatant material, a very natural slow-sinking bait can be arranged, which can be cast out and then allowed to drift slowly to the bottom on a line completely unhampered by float or lead weights of any kind. Hang on to the rod firmly and watch the line closely where it enters the water, as the 'takes' from fish when using such a hook offering can be most unexpected and savage. The danger point seems to be reached just after the cast has been made as the bait commences to sink. Perhaps the splash causes the bottom-lurking bass suddenly to become active and shoot rapidly surfacewards to intercept the fishy meal just as it begins its slow descent. When fishing this method do not be surprised, should you feel rather indolent and the day is hot and you fail to reel in at intervals to re-cast, to find that an out-size conger eel has gently sampled your bait and is trickling the line steadily off your reel against the ratchet on a centre-pin, the 'Tru-play' on a multiplier, or from the open free spool (with bale arm off) of your fixed-spool reel. It is doubtful if you will land such a formidable opponent on this 'gossamer' (for conger eels) tackle; but you will certainly have some hilarious moments immediately you strike and set the hook, until finally the line stretches, twangs taut and then is snapped like a piece of button thread.

Other Locations and Tackle

Some areas of our coastline are heavily indented with river mouths, estuaries or a maze of shallow, muddy creeks that are rich in marine life which attracts lots of foraging fish when the tide rises and floods the rich picking grounds where flocks of seabirds and shoreline waders find food at low water. The south-east coast (notably Essex) is particularly well endowed with such geographical features and, from the shorecaster's point of view, they have a twofold advantage in that they are so vast as to remain completely uncrowded even during the holiday season. They are also wonderful rough weather venues when the more open coast of the beaches and rock marks are unfishable owing to high winds and mountainous seas. Inside these sheltered marinas or tidal lagoons it is possible completely to beat the outside weather conditions and find some peaceful, productive angling for a great number of saltwater species which seem to lead a to-and-fro, double existence evenly divided between the genuine rolling 'blue water' deeps and the very quiet and food-providing seclusion of these tidal havens.

According to the power of the tide and the fish which are liable to be taken, a whole collection of different tackle rigs can be called into use to deal effectively with such a wealth of shorecasting situations. For the biggest of the tackle testers – cod, tope, dogfish or smooth-hounds – traditional beach fishing tackle can be employed if long casting with heavy leads is necessary. However it always pays to experiment in these inland waters, as the deep gullies with a very fast run of tide are not always the places which harbour the fish. Quite often mud-flats which have only a few feet of water over them will produce double figure cod, large bass and a selection of weighty lesser members of the shark family.

Some estuaries seem to have a resident shoal of mullet, flounders and 'school' bass in the 2 or 3 lb. range which move up and down with the tide and rarely, if ever, venture out into the wide open sea. Bait is usually no problem in these areas, as prolific lug and ragworm beds are often part and parcel of the landscape, as well as some of the best soft-crab collecting areas and shellfish gathering grounds.

The sheltered waters of estuaries which are very broad, so that there is never any really rough surf or broken water, just a gentle creeping up and down of the tide over extensive areas of mudflats, sandy gullies and weed-covered rock, are either the breeding ground or nursery of a multitude of small fish and marine aquatic life. Therefore it is quite natural that all kinds of predatory species, and crustacea and worm-devouring fish should congregate in these places. The astute shorecaster, by taking time off to study such fishy environments, will benefit greatly after such periods of observation when he takes up his tackle to put in some fishing sessions.

On crowded beaches or piers, when the angling is hectic and just one rod is sufficient to occupy any shorecaster, no matter how competent, I would never ever suggest 'doubling up' and using two sets of gear. Quiet-water estuary fishing is a totally different brand of angling activity, and where it is possible to be in sole command (another disastrous angling pun!) of the shoreline, a pair of rods can be set up; but to obtain the greatest experimental value from them, the rigs should be very dissimilar and totally different kinds of bait ought to be offered. The heavy gear designed for tope, cod, 'smoothies' or dogfish, can be the regular beachfishing outfit of 12 ft. rod, casting leads up to 6 oz., a multiplier capable of holding at least three hundred yards of (about) 20 lb. line and, most important, a 3 or 4 ft. cable-laid steel wire trace terminating in a sound forged 6/0 (or at the most) 8/0 hook with a well-honed point.

The supreme bait for estuary tope, especially over mud and sand, is the 'rolled flatfish': a 5 or 6 in. sand dab or flounder is beheaded and sliced centrally down the dark side, from top to tail, through to the back-bone. It can then be doubled over around the hook shank with the attractive white side showing and secured firmly at the root of the tail, just above the hook eye and twice down the body, with a few turns of soft, thin string. If this bait is cast well out and the rod mounted in a reliable monopod, with the reel left on a light 'check' setting, an audible warning will be given when a run develops.

Your second line of armoury can consist of a much lighter set of tackle in the very minimum casting weight beachcaster range – or even a 10ft. carp or pike, bait-casting rod, used in conjunction with a small multiplier, a fixed-spool reel or, if you fancy one, a small sea-size side-cast reel; all taking about 300 yards of 10 lb. line. It normally pays to ring the changes with terminal tackle and bait sizes when fishing a new and untried venue, and the whole idea behind a two rod set-up is versatility until some established fish feeding patterns have been discovered and some consistent catches made.

Over muddy, weedy, rock-strewn 'crabby' ground, peeler-crab is obviously the bait to commence fishing with on this light tackle rig; but plenty of alternative hook offerings should be tried, each in turn, so that a stereotyped 'one bait' angling habit is not developed. This habit is hard to break, especially if quite a few fish have been taken, which is apt to bring about a firm conviction that no other hook offering will prove of even the slightest interest to your quarry. The logic behind this thinking is most decidedly shaky, but I know legions of anglers who develop a one-bait habit which they refuse to break – and their catches suffer because of it.

If you commence your cod catching career with lugworm, and over a number of years catch plenty of fish on it, no doubt you will develop a strong feeling that it is a really good cod bait – which it most certainly is. However, should you allow your mental processes to proceed just one step farther, whereby you develop a fixation that as you have caught all your cod on lug it is the only bait that will take them. Then you are on shaky ground, because if you think clearly you will realise that the reason you have caught no cod on other baits is simply because you *have never used any!*

To depart for a paragraph or two from the powerful rods, strong lines and heavy lead techniques. Let us approach the true domain of the 'coarse-fisher-turned-shorecaster' and dwell for a little while upon certain methods of shorefishing for saltwater species which have taken up residence temporarily in an almost freshwater location, or alternatively, have moved with the tides up and down rivers, into harbours, or become trapped at low water in sea-fed lagoons until the tide rises again and allows them to return to their natural habitat – the sea.

At the outset, when considering such fishing, I would stress that without altering his tackle or even adding just one single small item, a coarse fisherman with a comprehensive set of equipment can, if he picks his locations and methods of angling carefully, take a great number of sea fish with the gear he already possesses. School bass (those about 2–3 lb.) and harbour or estuary mullet are the immediate quarry which spring to my mind; but there are also many others which can be taken from quiet, sheltered waters. Flounders and plaice can be caught in the traditional coarse fisher's style from a basket seat with float tackle and small garden worms or bunches of tiny ragworm, along the banks of tidal rivers where a gentle flow allows the flood to creep in and create just sufficient disturbance to colour the water and wash along all the many minute food offerings which set these 'flatties' feeding madly.

That very deadly long-distance float fishing method known as 'long-trotting' or 'trotting the stream' can be employed to good effect where ultra-shy mullet demand a fine tackle, and 'far-off' technique. At times, these fish shoal just out of casting range. If light tackle is being used and the temptation to use heavier gear and sufficient lead to reach them is succumbed to, the added disturbance of the rather weighty terminal rig as it splashes down amongst them instantly puts them on guard or causes them to flee altogether. With a soundly balanced coarse fishing set-up, if the angler carefully positions himself so that the current, tide or surface drift is in their direction, a very subtle bait presentation can be made by allowing the tackle to approach them in an undisturbed, natural fashion with the bait wavering around in front of a delicately 'held-back' float.

The 'baited-spoon' method of fishing for flounders is a widely publicised sea angling style, but how many harbour and estuary fishermen think of it in terms other than as used from a boat anchored in the tideway or being rowed with the spoon 'trolled' behind? A float fished 'baited-spoon' can prove very deadly indeed if the correct technique is used. The tackle is cast out and retrieved against the current in rather spasmodic flutters and jerks so that the spoon, with trailing baited

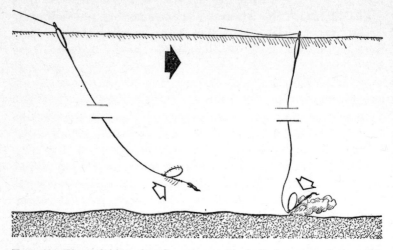

FIG. 41. Float fishing for flounders with baited spoon. *Left:* with float held back the spoon rises and flutters above the bottom. *Right:* float allowed to run freely – spoon dives to bottom sending up spurts of mud and sand. Large black arrow indicates tidal flow of current.

hook attached, alternately hovers above the bottom, and then dives into the sand or mud and raises little spurts or puffs of bottom sediment. To vary the technique it can also be 'long-trotted' down with the current, all the while 'holding-back' so that with the float supporting it, the baited-spoon flutters and wavers in the current and then drops back downstream a foot or so again.

Mudflats

What is commonly known in shorecasting parlance as 'mud-sploshing' can often be a very productive method of following the tide up an down over mudflats while fishing with both heavy beachcasting tackle (if the tidal flow is strong) or perhaps using the very lightest of gear where the angling is done in quiet tidal backwaters or lagoons, I am firmly convinced that more anglers do not take to this kind of shorefishing than the few who do, and really enjoy it immensely, simply because it is always a very messy business which quickly changes 'natty fishing wear' into the most disreputable 'tramp-type' garments.

The first and most important requirement of mud-crawling is that you shall have a most intimate knowledge of the stuff through which you will be ploughing – namely the mud. You should know its depth, what is underneath it, if it has deep 'pockets' which could totally engulf an unwary angler, how fast you can retreat over it before a rising tide and last, but vital if you wish to stay alive and fish to a ripe old age, the areas to steer clear of as being only suitable for birds which can take to the air to get themselves out of difficulty.

Before you venture out upon the mud with your tackle, you must realise that – unlike the shorelines composed of sand, rock or gravel – on the mud there is nowhere suitable to put anything down unless you take some form of receptacle which will carry all the gear which you normally dump on the beach. A further important stipulation also, whatever it is you put your gear into *must float* – but not be carried away should you be engaged with a fish as the tide rises a few inches around you. After many experiments, I can thoroughly recommend a polythene baby bath; one about 30 in. long, 18 in. wide and 8–10 in. deep. At one end there is usually a flat projecting soap shelf with a hole in it for hanging up the bath. Take note regarding that hole. It is most important as it can be slotted with a strong piece of cord to which a stake or a metal rod is attached, so that the bath, with your precious bait, lunch, camera and tackle bag in it can be firmly tethered when the stake is driven into the mud. At a pinch, if the tide is rising fast when you are retreating before it with rod in hand, the bath with all your tackle in it can be dragged over the mud by the cord. And finally; what a wonderful fish container the baby bath makes for the boot of your car. The rest of your gear is not plastered with blood and slime should you absentmindedly throw in a great bunch of wet, mud-and-sand splattered fish, as you hurriedly jump in and drive off home.

I feel quite sure that the reason why some anglers find fishing on mud-flats so attractive is because such locations, by their very messy, hard to approach, rather dangerous nature, do not attract the hoards of 'clean foot operators' who prefer to drive right up to their casting positions and thereby expend the minimum amount of energy.

Artificial Means of Food Attraction

If you are a coarse fisherman who has recently become enamoured of sea angling and you are fortunate enough to have built up over the years an armoury of rods, which include perhaps a couple for pike spinning, together with one of those great cantilever boxes with a multitude of compartments all filled with lures of all shapes, designs and sizes, then a further branch of shorecasting will immediately be opened up to you. The attractions are primarily that it is an all-action branch of the saltwater scene which happily does not demand the constant provision of bait, which relieves your pocket of expense or your back of strain – according to whether you buy or dig it!

It is generally accepted that about three or four species: bass, pollack, mackerel and coalfish, can readily be taken from suitable shore marks which give on to reasonably clear, deep water by employing what I would describe as artificial means of food attraction. No hard-and-fast rules, however can be made when considering what species of fish will or will not accept such mechanically imitative forms of lure. For years it was thought that the real grandads of the cod tribe could only be taken with very large, juicy natural baits; until the 'jig' or 'pirking' experts fishing deep water from small boats began to take forty-pound-plus cod on polished chromium taxi-cab door handles fitted with hooks and lengths of lead-filled metal tube highly burnished and fitted at the lower end with a treble hook!

I like spinning rods to have a rather 'soft', whippy action in order that the lightest line (preferably on a fixed-spool or small multiplier reel) can be used in conjunction with them. The reason is that quite a number of the fish you catch while spinning will 'hit' the lure with great force and at a considerable speed as it is being retrieved, and the sudden, powerful wrench which is felt on such an occasion would immediately snap (say) an 8 or 10 lb. line if it was being used with a rod with an unyielding, poker-like action. The length of the rod, if it is to be used for spinning from rock marks or steep-to beaches, should be about 9–10 ft., so that adequate control over a fish when it is close in is possible. A very short rod in the 6 ft. range, while suitable for boat angling where there is clear water all around will have insufficient length to enable you to steer a good lively fish over clumps of weed or around barnacle-encrusted tongues of outjutting rock when it has been brought close in, and is at the dangerous stage of being on a very short line immediately before landing.

To obtain a most attractive 'fish-like' retrieve of your lure when spinning, it pays to vary the speed at which it comes back towards you through the water (small fish hardly swim straight and fast like cars on a motorway) and also to avoid, as far as possible, lots of cluttering gadgets mounted up the line which precede your articifical offering like the strung-out contents of a tackle shop drawer! At times I have seen anglers fishing in very clear water on bright days, when every frond of bottom weed was visible, with a couple of gleaming brass swivels, three anti-kink leads, and finally a very small spoon which was completely dwarfed by the assorted ironmongery which travelled before it and completely put off any fish which may have been inclined to have a go at it. In order to keep the bits and pieces down to the bare minimum when spinning, go every time for spinning lures with a built-in casting weight, and above all, if they are fitted with cheap, nasty swivels which do not work, discard them and fit all your spinners with the more expensive, but totally reliable, ball-bearing swivels which really do revolve quite freely. As an afterthought, if you are spinning on a strict budget, just buy two or three, and fit one to the spinners as you use them with either a split ring or a link swivel attachment.

Piers and Harbour Walls

Let me here and now confess that while I personally am not a lover of pier and harbour-wall fishing due to the rather hair-raising (and I mean that literally) casting antics of some aspiring shorefishers, it can be a most comfortable and sometimes vastly rewarding branch of shorecasting which affords very easy access for those who are far from young, and for those at the other end of the age scale, too. Some parents, who would never allow their youngsters out on lonely shorelines, do not mind in the least, and feel quite easy in their minds, if their fishing-mad offspring spends the whole of his leisure time on the local pier, jetty, or harbour wall, happily performing miracles of fish catching with a rod and line, where lots of adults are present should he get into any kind of difficulty.

On my travels, I am positive that I have seen just about every single item of coarse, sea, and even game, fishing tackle being used from pier or harbour walls, some of it by intention being used to good effect; and other items, such as light match rods being severaly punished by casting 3 oz. weights; merely because the unfortunate operator had no suitable gear to fish with. In extreme circumstances, I would say that most types of rods and reels can be called into service for pier fishing provided they are not asked to do a job for which they are either too frail or, alternatively, too robust. The ideal pier rod in my estimation is about 8–9 ft. long and needs to be quite powerful if long 'haul-ups' from water level are necessary, unless a drop-net (a landing net on a long rope) is used continually to land the heavyweights. Even so, on lots of occasions there is an abiding temptation to winch up anything under about 10 lb., especially if you are fishing alone at night and a dropnet operator is not within hailing distance. Unless you wish to indulge in prolonged bouts of beach-style long casting (on which subject I have strong feelings) your medium length pier rod can be fitted with a large, sound centre-pin reel which will give a fast retrieve and lots of 'direct-pull', reeling-in power. Line strength can be a problem. For straight-sided harbour walls with snag-free bottoms, something in the region of 10–20 lb. can be adequate. Conversely, around piers with girders and underwater rails, where big fish are apt to be caught which have to be held tight to keep them away from the tackle tangling ironwork, perhaps a breaking strain in the region of 30 lb. would be sensible.

Whilst the traditional pier fishing terminal tackle has for years been a 'Christmas tree' paternoster rig of 'grip' lead above which project three or four brass booms with short hook snoods, happily, within the last decade, truly enlightened pier anglers have for the most part dispensed with such 'haul 'em up in strings' rigs, and have designed both leger and paternoster tackles which incorporate just one, or at the most two, hooks.

Congering

Finally, after considering all these different types of shore-casting locations and methods, let me, specifically for those adventurous souls who love excitement and a little danger to add spice to their fishing, recommend congering from the rocks, piers or harbour walls during the hours of darkness. This is the time when these fearsome, serpentine creatures are most active. It is definitely a warm, calm sea, windless night pursuit; for the angler must play a sit-and-wait game in the darkness with his reel on a very light audible 'check' setting which will in no way retard the free passage of the line from the reel and at the same time, put him into a state of nerve-tingling anticipation and readiness.

The tackle must be powerful. Note: I did not say cumbersome. A really sound beachcaster intended to cast heavy leads or a 'big fish' boat rod will be adequate, and it must be coupled up with a rugged single action centre-pin reel or a big multiplier carrying a loading of very sound, reliable non-stretch line. It is foolish to attempt sporty tactics with congers; so use a good braided nylon, terylene or dacron line somewhere in the 60, 70 or even 80 lb. b.s. range, according to the snagging possibilities of the shoreline. Heavy leads will mean many false runs as the eels gently investigate the bait before mouthing it, and even then a little more time will have to be given them before they move off purposefully and a strike can be made. This 'when to strike' dilemma in shore congering can be a real problem. Too soon and the bait is pulled from the eel's mouth, too late and it has become safely ensconced in its rocky, underwater funk-hole from whence it cannot be pulled even if you engaged a tug-of-war team!

As I have stressed previously, of all the fish which the shorecaster is likely to encounter, the conger is the most formidable both in and out of water. For landing gear, the ordinary screw-in-head type of gaff is useless as a 'conger-nobbler'. Nothing but an immensely strong, fixed-head, one-piece instrument should be used. Preferably this should be in the hands of an unemotional, fearless, heavyweight angling companion with both (thickly gloved) hands free to operate it, and a headlight strapped on so that he can be absolutely sure where he is sticking the gaff hook should you, the angler with the rod, get into the dangerous position of being between him and the fish.

You will certainly find plenty of excitement and lots of hilarity when shore congering at night, but in conclusion, let me offer a few words of warning. At all costs never make the fatal mistake of presuming that a conger eel is dead and poke around near its head with either your hands or feet, even if they are thickly gloved or booted. Also, should the situation with a very large eel get completely out of hand, don't be afraid to cut the line and retreat in safety, rather than emerge from the fray a very brave, but fingerless hero!

When fishing from the shore it is possible to practise evasive action to save becoming a hospital casualty requiring extensive surgery. Bear in mind the age-old story of the two anglers fishing for conger from a small boat. When one of them hooked a real 'rod-bender' and after much sweating and straining brought it up to the surface and prepared to heave it inboard, his companion jumped up, and after removing his heavy coat and boots, stated very sincerely: 'If that thing comes in here ... I'm definitely going over the side ... I will be much safer there!'

Index

Index

Figures in italics denote illustrations.